ENDOR

A desperately needed perspective on the nature of Christian leadership. Kirlin articulates well the need for courage that is deeply rooted in one's identity in Christ. This courage causes us to lead both passionately and boldly. *Leadership Courage* is a must read for current pastors and those who are feeling a call to the ministry.

Rev. Dr. Dana S. Allin, Synod Executive ECO: A Covenant Order of Evangelical Presbyterians, Goleta, CA

Kirk Kirlin loves the church and its pastors. And because of this love, he grieves over the state of the church. Having lost its distinctiveness, having compromised and capitulated to the culture around it, having lost its call to be salt and light, he passionately summons pastors back to courageous leadership. Through nine powerful leadership distinctives, Kirk shows pastors how they can lead with courage, conviction and compassion, helping restore the church's distinctiveness and impact both in the lives of individual members and the community. *Leadership Courage* is an empowering book that will help pastors tremendously. I hope it is read widely.

Jim Belcher, President Providence Christian College, Pasadena, CA and author of *Deep Church* and *In Search of Deep Faith*

What is courage? Is it fearlessness? No. It's being scared out of your wits and going ahead anyway. In his new book, *Leadership Courage*, coach and consultant Kirk Kirlin has penned the powerful, life-giving words every leader needs to read, reread, and read again, so they too can find the means to prevail when they want to give up, continue when they want to quit, and move forward when they'd rather stay right where they are.

Forged in the crucible of experience of multiple leadership capacities and coaching leaders of all kinds in many different fields, Kirk helps his readers face their fears, overcome their obstacles and summon the fortitude they need to no longer be held captive to those things which paralyze their actions.

Kirk's experience shines through every page of this thoughtful, well organized, and catalyzing resource with biblical insights, practical applications, and real-world illustrations. Importantly, he continuously points to the source of real courage…total surrender to the Captain of Our Souls, Jesus Christ.

Eminently readable, utterly practical, and immediately implementable this book will become one of your go to, dog-eared, underlined and post it noted resources. *Leadership Courage* needs to be in the hands of everyone wanting to make a difference in their world today.

Tom Clegg, President and Founder, The Clegg Consulting
Group and author of *Lost in America, Missing in America,*
and *Releasing your Church's Potential*

In a day where leadership has become a pecking order it is refreshing to see a work about leaders finding their unique Jesus style and creating synergy, partnership and movement within the mission of God. Kirk Kirlin has nailed the latter and you are the beneficiary.

Kirk has seen it all and now uses those observations to help us develop a 360° view of leadership on mission instead of leadership as vocation. Read *Leadership Courage*, reflect, and then replace anything unnecessary with the necessity of the Jesus style.

Alan Hirsch, missiologist, futurist, and author of *5Q: Reactivating the Original Intelligence and Capacity of the Body of Christ* and *The Forgotten Ways*; co-author of *The Shaping of Things to Come*, Alan is founder of 5Q Collective and Forge

Kirk Kirlin brings decades of experience in the trenches of the North American church to *Leadership Courage*. Provocative. Prophetic. Powerful. The book is a clarion call to "step up and further in" for those committed to serious leadership, which is the crisis of the age in which we live.

Don't immerse yourself in these pages unless you are willing to be stretched and uncomfortable. This is not a volume for those who want inspirational pablum, rather for those who are deeply serious about leadership and North American Christianity.

Sam Metcalf, President of Novo Mission and author of *Beyond the Local Church: How Apostolic Movements Can Change the World*

A learner does not have to search very long to find books, articles, and blogs on the topic of leadership. There seems to be no question about the importance of leadership to every organization. It is vital for organizations to achieve success and to fulfill their mission. The courage part of leadership is not a common topic, but Kirk Kirlin personally knows the value of courageous leadership.

When Kirk first published the content of this book in weekly blogs it was imperative for me to save the blogs and share them with pastors and leaders who were in need. The blog postings were a starting point. Now with the publishing of *Leadership Courage* everyone can benefit from the importance, encouragement and challenge of being a courageous leader.

This book will change the culture of your organization and point you in the needed direction to be effective and faithful to your mission. As you read you will begin to apply the principles in your area of responsibility, and others will benefit.

Gary Norton, Facilitator for Revitalization Pacific Southwest
District, The Lutheran Church-Missouri Synod

Leadership Courage is both relevant and cutting edge. It is well written, captivating, and challenging. It constantly gets to the heart of pastoral ministry and calls leaders to engage with their pioneers to reach the community with the love of Christ through service. Jesus' church needs missional leaders willing to take the church out of the comfort zones of self-interest into the space of spending ourselves for the cause of Christ.

Leadership Courage calls pastors and leaders back to the mission of Jesus in a way I haven't seen in any other book. Written as a coaching tool, a pastor and his or her team can use it to make changes in the way their church operates.

Get this book into the hands of your colleagues and church members as quickly as you can.

Pastor Neil Thompson, Ministerial Association Secretary
North New South Wales Conference of the Seventh-day Adventist
Church, Australia

Leadership Courage begins with Kirk Kirlin telling his pastoral story. From naive upstart to wounded warrior to fearful functionary and finally to the courageous leadership that comes from rediscovering our worth in Christ.

Did the first stages in his story sound familiar to you? They did for me. They resonate with more pastors than we'd like to admit – even to ourselves.

If you've ever been hurt while trying to be faithful in church leadership, if you feel stuck in fear, helplessness, or hopelessness, unsure of how to become the courageous leader you were meant to be, I recommend *Leadership Courage* to you. Filled with practical, biblical principles, it can help you rediscover the biblical courage you and your congregation need – and your heart has been longing for.

Karl Vaters, Pastor and author of *The Grasshopper Myth, Small Church Essentials*, and *100 Days to a Healthier Church*. Helping Small Churches Thrive at KarlVaters.com

Oh, how I wish this book had been around when I was beginning pastoral ministry twenty-five years ago! Kirk Kirlin's bracing, inspiring challenge to church leaders to "move forward in the face of fear" hits us where we live.

With short, readable chapters so refreshingly honest about what it means to lead, and yet filled with faith in God's ability to equip us, *Leadership Courage* is great for someone just entering the ministry, or as a mid-course renewal for a leader who is discouraged or complacent.

Dr. Jeff Berger, Senior Pastor, First Baptist, Conroe, TX
Author of *Finding Jesus*

I have known Kirk Kirlin as a friend, coach, and mentor since 2003. *Leadership Courage* is the essence of who he is. This book is not leadership theory but rather a raw challenge to the status quo for all who serve in church leadership at any level.

Leadership Courage should be required reading for all pastors and elders serving in the local church. May God grant us the courage to lead with our hearts "all in!"

Gary A. Brady, Lead Pastor and Denominational Executive
Visalia Adventist Church, CA

Every effective pastor and business executive will benefit from a leadership coach. Kirk Kirlin "impacts the impactors" with great insight and life-changing principles. As I read *Leadership Courage* I felt like I had Kirk in my living room helping me through so many of the issues I face as a leader. This book is practical, compelling and challenging.

Jim Burns, PhD, President, HomeWord,
and author of *Doing Life With Your Adult Child: Keep Your Mouth Shut and the Welcome Mat Out*

Kirk Kirlin's book, *Leadership Courage*, is long overdue. It is not a theological text. Neither is it a book about church growth. It deals with the internal workings of pastors and other Christian leaders. It deals with matters of the soul which are profoundly spiritual, yet which don't sound spiritual. For this reason, they are often overlooked.

In this book, Kirk places his finger on one of the most pervasive —yet unrecognized and therefore undiscussed—issues in modern American church life. For most, the symptoms will be familiar yet hazy. He brings them into focus by painting a compelling portrait of the various facets of the failure of leadership, and he then describes what healthy leadership looks like and how to develop it.

Ken Fish, Founder, Kingdom Fire Ministries

Leaders take responsibility. In *Leadership Courage*, Kirk Kirlin challenges us to take full responsibility—courageously—for the right things. Courage is a verb for leaders. It's finding the signature Jesus has written over my life and embracing His grace in obedience to His call. Kirk invites us "to live and lead with your heart fully engaged." When engagement is based on alignment that flows from intimacy with and dependence on Jesus, it creates what some call "spiritual grit," or courage.

This is not a book to be read alone. Gather a cohort, work through the discussion questions at the end of each chapter. Allow the Spirit to create a humble authenticity that challenges others to follow.

Steve Hopkins, State Convention of Baptists in Ohio

Leadership Courage is a home run! It is the best book in years for churches on a most vital issue...LEADERSHIP. Drawing from the outstanding book by Edwin Friedman, *A Failure Of Nerve*, it addresses the dilemma of weak, ineffective leadership within the church. Even better, the book goes on to give practical, workable solutions for those of us who are leading.

Happy Leman, Founding Pastor Vineyard Church of Central Illinois, National Vineyard Leader/Board Member

I know of no leader who is better able to cultivate courage in the lives of leaders. Kirk is a master coach and now he has translated his own experience into a masterclass on the nature of courage and the way it transforms ministry leadership.

Accessible. Anchored in reality. Provocative. Dangerous. This book is not for the faint of heart. You cannot read it without being disturbed by some of the ways your own leadership has been compromised. However, with one insight after another, Kirk not only exposes the patterns that sabotage our impact, he calls out a new level of courage. *This* is the leadership development course we all needed—the course I needed—but nobody offered. I would go so far as to say, every leader I know should not just read this book, but also find the courage to process the reflection assignments in each chapter.

> Dr. Gary R. Mayes, Executive Director of ChurchNEXT,
> and author of *DNA of a Revolution* and *Now What?*

What is lacking for most church leaders today is not more information or programmatic savvy…what is missing is the courage to really lead. Creatively drawing from the wisdom of Edwin Friedman's *A Failure of Nerve*, Kirk exposes the most common contributors to this condition and offers the reader both biblical and contemporary examples and principles that can help leaders overcome the predominant North American church culture of cowardice.

I loved his description of what he calls *pioneers, belongers* and *resisters* who are found in most every church setting. "Contrary to almost everything you've ever read about leadership, I want to assert, that a great leader is not one who somehow inspires 'belongers' to become 'pioneers,' or 'resisters' to transform into 'belongers.' No. A great leader is one who leads her or his people appropriately." After teasing out the differences between these three types of people, Kirk urges church leaders to stop focusing their efforts on those least motivated to follow their game-changing leadership vision and example. "Work to clear your calendar of resisters, and to fill it with pioneers...with those who are most responsive to your leadership." No doubt, a courageous move!

Later he writes, "Consider how little the church asks of Christians—in the name of 'grace.'" I also was intrigued with Kirk's emphasis on the American Church's safer, more comfortable paradigm of a two-fold (pastor/teacher) leadership profile, rather than the more courageous, five-fold paradigm described in Ephesians 4 which produces mature disciples of Jesus. He writes, "And when the apostolic is missing, minimized, or marginalized, you get, well...you get what we have today."

My hope is that *Leadership Courage* gets into the hands of many church leaders across the country and beyond as I believe the Spirit of God can use it to powerfully expose and inspire the body of Christ to rise up once again with courageous obedience to make more and better disciples of Jesus and advance his Kingdom. It's time for a courage awakening!

Dr. Bill Randall, Director of Novo/Pioneering Initiatives
and author of *The Life Jesus Made Possible: Embracing the Kingdom
Within Our Reach*

After forty years of pastoral ministry, reading *Leadership Courage* has challenged me to paint my face like William Wallace, grip my sword, and run back into the battle with a renewed heart of courage. This book will make you uncomfortable and provoke you to stop playing it safe and risk it all to follow the Master into the adventure of leadership.

With the clarion call of a prophet and a contrarian's flip-the-tables approach, Kirk Kirlin challenges status quo assumptions and practices of the capital "C" Church. Not just content to richly share his own vulnerabilities and insights, Kirlin includes rich personal reflective exercises and group discussion questions to probe motivations and values. Ready to have your worldview driven to new vistas?—fasten your seatbelts with *Leadership Courage*!

Leadership Courage has been transformational for me individually and for our church. Applying its concepts and principles helped us make the difficult switch "from maintenance to mission." As a result, our church became missionally influential in our community. These distinctions have also been life-changing for me personally. I've grown in courage, clarity, and confidence as a pastor, Christ-follower, husband, father, and people-developer.

I recommend *Leadership Courage* to any pastor who wants to become the kind of Christian who provokes maturity in those around him or her.

Kirk Kirlin has had a profound impact on hundreds of leaders because he walks the walk. *Leadership Courage* is not theory; this is a book about the real issues of leadership: character, inner fortitude, courage, and identity. For those walking through the fires of life and leadership, this book will be a forge that helps shape your soul.

Brandon Cook, Pastor of Vision and Teaching, Long Beach Christian Fellowship and author of *Learning to Live and Love Like Jesus* and *The Cost of Cheap Grace: Reclaiming the Value of Discipleship*

Kirk Kirlin nails it! The church needs a new reformation. A reformation of what it means to lead courageously in a consumer-saturated culture. The church and its leadership is being challenged once again, as in the days of the book of Acts, to bend to a "culture of cowardice."

What we need are strong leaders who are willing to lead courageously. As he led God's people into the promised land, ten times God told Joshua to be "strong and courageous." As a lead pastor and local church leader I am constantly challenged to lead courageously with my heart and not just my head.

Unlike many leadership books, *Leadership Courage* is a gold mine of wisdom derived from Kirk's years of experience working with local pastors and leaders of which I have been the beneficiary. This book will challenge you and your teams become leaders like Joshua. This is a must read for every pastor and leader who isn't satisfied being on the banks of the promised land but is ready to lead yourself, your family, and your church courageously into all God has promised you.

Lance Dannic, Lead Pastor, Hope Church, Kalispell MT

Laura and I have been impacted by Kirk Kirlin & his wife Dr. Annie in incalculable ways! From introducing me to Laura, to facilitating our pre-marital counseling, personal, and business coaching, we trust the Kirlin's with the most intimate parts of our lives.

Leadership Courage is a must read for the bold leader who is tired of the status quo, and longs to reach the next level. It is packed with pearls of wisdom and insight!

Ryan Dobson, President of REBEL Parenting

Amazing! This is one of the best books I have read regarding leadership development. *Leadership Courage* is direct and to the point without any sugarcoating. Kirk does an amazing job of bringing his life experience, combined with years of research, to help the reader understand what life could be like as a true disciple of Christ.

For any organization brave enough to read it, this book will change the future of your team while expanding the Kingdom of God. It is so refreshing to read a work that encourages you to take risks while trusting God and living life with passion and purpose!

Jim Duran, Lead Pastor, The River Community Church,
Ventura, CA

As a church planter and pastor in my early 30's I can't recommend *Leadership Courage* enough. Kirk Kirlin is not only an excellent leadership teacher but he is rich in experience as well.

The leadership principles in his book are timeless and relevant no matter what season of leadership you find yourself in. Whether you're in business, leading a thriving non-profit, or pastoring a local church

Leadership Courage is for you.

Joe Pena, Founder, Relentless Church, Las Vegas, NV

In *Leadership Courage* Kirk Kirlin coaches and coaxes out the primary character trait missing in North American Christians today: the courage to respond to the Father's call. It is primarily due Kirk's influence on my life that I pray nightly for this courage in each of my children.

Jay Schroder, Local Missions Partners Team Leader,
Southeast Christian Church, Louisville, KY

There are leaders who want you to look up to them and there are leaders who look down on you. Then, there are the godly leaders who sit beside you and stand behind you as they nudge you forward in your calling, effectiveness and impact in the Kingdom work of God. Kirk Kirlin is this partner leader. His new book, *Leadership Courage*, takes a deep breath and then confronts the accepted ways in favor of the godly ways of love, service, and empowerment to the Body of Christ.

Borrowing the words of Eugene Peterson, I would encourage you to "eat this book" and let it become food for your work as a servant leader in the mold of Jesus.

Phil Underwood, Pastor and Mission Facilitator, Bluewater in the Keys, Islamorada, FL and author of *Shift: Gearing Your Heart to Lead God's Mission*

Leadership Courage is a wake up for church leaders to stop playing it safe and to lead with their hearts fully engaged. As a pastor, I appreciate the reminder that who I am speaks more loudly than anything I say. If you have a leadership role in the church, then I dare you to take Kirk's insights seriously. You and the people you lead will be grateful you did.

Eric Wayman, Lead Pastor, Lighthouse Community Church, Costa Mesa, CA and author of *Reclaiming Your Identity*

LEADERSHIP COURAGE

Leadership in a Culture of Cowardice

Kirk Kirlin

AUTHORS PLACE
—PRESS—

Published by Authors Place Press
9885 Wyecliff Drive, Suite 200
Highlands Ranch, CO 80126
Authorsplace.com

Manufactured in the United States of America.

ISBN: 978-1-62865-756-2

Contents

—————

Introduction. 19

How to Read This Book. 32

PART ONE

THE HEART OF THE MATTER

CHAPTER 1

The *Heart* to Lead – Living Courageously 35

CHAPTER 2

The Price of Love 46

PART TWO

THE CONDITION OF THE CHURCH

CHAPTER 3

A Culture of Cowardice 56

CHAPTER 4

The Challenge of Change. 66

PART THREE

PRINCIPLES OF LEADERSHIP COURAGE

CHAPTER 5

Presence 79

CHAPTER 6

Responsibility 89

CHAPTER 7

Differentiation 96

CHAPTER 8

Stand 101

CHAPTER 9

Motivation 109

CHAPTER 10

The Adventurous Life 123

CHAPTER 11

Undermine the 80/20 Rule 136

CHAPTER 12

The Unreasonableness of Being Reasonable 149

CHAPTER 13

Go First! 161

PART FOUR

CODA

In Conclusion 209

Leadership Courage Bibliography 210

Introduction

My dad was a courageous man. At 89, he prayed to receive Christ and lived the last eight years of his life as one of the kindest souls you could ever meet. He told me a story about growing up and how he almost died that I've never forgotten.

When a teenager, my dad convinced two of his buddies to abandon a guided tour in Kentucky's Mammoth Cave to explore on their own. When their lantern went out, they were forced to feel their way through the blackness, hands on the cave walls.

At one point the walls on either side began to gradually widen. Instinctively, my dad widened his stance, spreading his feet as he shuffled forward. Suddenly, two simultaneous sensations terrified him. A dank updraft washed across his face *from between his legs* and he heard the sound of pebbles he dislodged with his boot as they fell soundlessly for long seconds before striking a rock surface hundreds of feet below! Moving without seeing, my dad and his friends were inches from death. Miraculously, they were able to shuffle backward, somehow retracing their steps, and eventually reunited with their tour group.

One of the reasons this story has stuck with me is because it's sort of a metaphor for my own life. I've lived through several precarious times with no guarantee of success or safety. Maybe you've had your own dangerous experiences, or maybe you've aimed to plan your life so well as to *avoid* danger altogether!

What's universally true in life though, is that danger, risk, and uncertainty are inevitable *especially* for followers of Jesus. I've learned these lessons first-hand through my experiences with family, in business, and especially in ministry.

The Uncertainty of Christian Life

My faith journey began early in my MBA program. From my teen years I'd been enthusiastically preparing to join my dad in the small manufacturing business started by his dad and grandad. The toughest part of the academic rigor was behind me: a bachelor's degree in electrical engineering. I was thriving in the stimulating practicality of business and management.

Within months of receiving Christ, I experienced a clear and compelling call to the ministry. In time, I understood that this meant I could not wholeheartedly devote myself to the company as my forebears had. For reasons that had more to do with simple obedience than anything about this particular business, I could not serve God *and* the company.

My parents, who were not Christ-followers at the time were incredulous. My dad flew to Logan Airport to confront the foolhardiness of my decision and to communicate just how severely I'd broken the hearts of my mother, grandmothers, and, by inference, my dad. It was an upsetting, emotional encounter. We parted unreconciled.

As I took the "T" back to my dorm, the Lord ministered to me. God comforted me with the knowledge that I had brooked this first significant test of my young faith and had come out with integrity intact. It would take decades for the relationship with my dad to be fully repaired. And, God was faithful to minister to each of us in that season. But that was just the beginning of a larger story I didn't know lay ahead of me in a life of ministry.

In one particular season of what seemed to be irrefutable confirmations, a small group of us became convinced we were to start a church together. As anyone who has been on the ground floor of a church plant can attest, the sacrifices of time, passion, money, energy, prayer, and just plain *work* are enormous. For three years the young ministry prospered and grew. New converts to Christ were delightfully commonplace.

Then, an affair took out two of our most gifted leaders. Chaos resulted. People scattered. The baby Christians fled—many left not only the church, but also their faith.

Annie and I were rocked. The affair had taken place right before our eyes, destroying the marriages of four of our closest friends. Blaming myself for not seeing what, in hindsight, was so obvious, I began to question my fitness for ministry. I began to doubt the call to ministry that God had so graciously made clear a decade before.

These, and dozens of experiences like them, have enticed me to restrain my optimism, moderate my belief in people, and truncate the openness with which I've chosen to relate to others. Several times now, Annie and I have made years-long commitments to ministries we deeply believed in and devoted ourselves to. When moral failures, personnel changes, demographic shifts, or strategic miscalculations brought these dreams to an often-abrupt ending, we have been tempted to self-protect.

Responding to my disillusionment, a friend urged me to read *The Making of a Leader* by Dr. J. Robert Clinton. I learned that God uses every event in a leader's life to shape her or him to become the person God intends. Nothing in life is wasted. Nothing is lost.

Like a tiny sprout, hope began to emerge from the dry soil of my heartsick self. God's Word ministered to me, and again, confident—not in my abilities, but in God's love for me—my faith was encouraged, and I began to see the possibility of fruitful ministry emerging from the encircling darkness. In time, God made our next steps clear, gave us grace for the next journey, and launched us into an exciting six-year ministry endeavor.

Maybe you're nodding in recognition to my stories as you think about your own trials in life. Maybe the stories seem foreign. However you relate, sharing these stories isn't meant to prop myself up, but to give you a backdrop for why I'm so driven to help Christian leaders succeed.

Getting through each of these trials was hard. Really hard. And it required courage from me that was only made possible through a sure hope in God and God's promises. Too often we Christians lose heart. I know there are times that I have.

Standing strong as a leader during those times required wholehearted courage that took a lot of time and heartache to develop. I hope to pass on what I've learned to you.

LEADERSHIP REQUIRES COURAGE

Leadership is, above all else, a matter of the heart. To lead courageously is an expensive proposition—just as expensive as love. C. S. Lewis said, *"To love at all is to be vulnerable. Love anything and your heart will be wrung and possibly broken."*

Lewis' quote could be applied to leadership as well. *To lead at all* is to be vulnerable. Lead any valuable endeavor and your heart will, at times, be wrung and possibly broken. Leading well requires that you have a healthy relationship with responsibility. Owning one's responsibilities takes courage.

And yet, I've observed that many in church leadership shrink back from healthy responsibility and instead embrace a "culture of cowardice" that I think can be traced – at least in part – to cultural shifts that those in the church have adopted. This culture makes courage even more rare *and* important.

Over the decades, I've noticed that American adults are prolonging their adolescence. Many delay completing college, avoid the commitment of marriage, live with their parents into their 20s and 30s, have historically low savings rates, and high levels of personal debt. To me, these are indicators that American society is less mature than it once was. As society has grown more childish, so has the Church.

But when those who hold the keys to power in our churches attempt to minimize the discomfort our members associate with change, they reinforce the juvenility that causes the Church to fail at just about everything *God* has called it to be and do. Change doesn't have to be a threat; it is an adventure that God calls Christian leaders to step into.

Yet, so often what we settle for in church life is shaped by our congregation members' demand for comfort, a comfort that may be precipitated in part by these broad cultural shifts. In many cases, pastors are expected to entertain, inform, soothe, and comfort the flock. American pastors are often caught in a race from bedside to living room in response to the mandate of their members to quell their every anxiety. In these circumstances, pastors are often held hostage by leadership boards, influential individuals, or small coalitions in their churches who wield exceptional power.

As a result, pastors are stymied in undertaking bold initiatives that require significant sacrifice on the part of the congregation. They are never to challenge, upset, or provoke their people. When they do—even when Scripture requires that they do—pastors are routinely attacked, opposed, and too often fired.

For pastors who aren't run out of town, often the incessant resistance to their leadership coaxes them to stifle or abandon the dreams God planted in their hearts. Instead, they scamper to palliate every bump and bruise their members' experience. The energy they have left is often consumed planning, preparing, and producing weekend services. It's not leading. At best, it's management. Rather than catalyzing life-giving change, they often end up producing and emceeing a weekly event.

Whether a weekly gathering involves hundreds of intricately choreographed parts, or is simple and rudimentary, the result is largely the same: lives are not changed and people live little differently as a result.

This is heartbreaking. I'm saddened by the life-sapping demands that burden so many of our pastors. In my view, they could be doing so much more productive work discipling leaders and impacting their communities. Instead, their vitality is consumed satiating every need of their congregations.

Convinced it doesn't have to be this way, I have a vision for something different.

The compulsion for the Church to retreat to the margins of society is ever present, especially now. For Christians and churches to bring a clear, distinctive, restorative, and visibly beneficial dynamism to society, our leaders will be heroic, God-trusting activists who live like those in Scripture whose example has inspired millions across history.

The Bible we read is *full* of examples of God's people trusting and moving into unknown, uncertain, or absolutely *dangerous* territory in response to God's direction. Responding as they did required an "all-in" commitment rarely seen today. It is my passion to champion Christian influencers to live their lives all-in.

If this vision calls to you, read on. But know, this vision can't come to fruition through a single leader, though it must begin there. Ultimately, it will take teams of dedicated, trusting, God-fearing, and humble leaders to pull this off. Integral to the success of the Church I see is teams of leaders who work with – not against – the lead pastor.

A Vision for Pastoral Leadership

I envision leadership teams where elders willingly follow their pastor's lead, launch innovative ministry that challenges the status quo, and demonstrate Gospel goodness to those who are yet to follow Jesus. In this kind of church, elders will be championing the pastor's pursuit of God, clearing obstacles from his or her path, and making resources available so the ministry can take God-authored leaps into the unprecedented. As they do, they'll *experience* God's faithfulness while growing in maturity.

When pastors are supported this way, they'll be freed to seek the Lord's direction, enroll a congregation postured to bring glory to God through their trusting obedience, and continually experiment with outward-moving ministry initiatives that brighten a gloomy world. Churches will be incubators of innovation and "no fault zones," where bold risks are as common as they are in the Book of Acts, and learning, growing, stretching and becoming is experienced. This growth and risk-taking can really only be experienced when pastors are freed to build other leaders.

In order to strengthen congregations and multiply leaders, church leadership teams must have a healthy, biblical view of what a pastor is and is not.

In my view, pastors are, first of all, followers of God. His or her pursuit of the Lord Jesus is primary.

Second, the pastor is a role model of the way one follows Jesus no matter what. Living as an exemplar requires proximity and access. Other than making time to pray in solitude, Jesus was *with* the disciples. [Mark 3:14]

Jesus' disciples spent much more time with him than most Western pastors spend with their people. Just imagine the impact on the three, the twelve, and the seventy-two if Jesus regularly retreated to his study twenty to thirty hours a week.

Third, a pastor is a people-developer. Pastors get to provoke those close to them to *grow in Christ-likeness.* As a people-developer, a pastor gets to dream up ways for their people to grow as apprentices of Jesus, beginning with those closest to them: their senior staff, elders, key leaders, and immediate family. These are the people with the proximity and access to readily be influenced by the pastor's life, leadership, and example.

When Jesus' disciples encountered hardships and threats, Jesus used these opportunities to propel them toward God in faith. He was careful not to cater to their preferences, assuage their anxieties, or diminish their distress. In most cases, Jesus challenged them to *greater* risk, trusting the Father. Because he did, they *experienced* God's rescue. As a result, they grew confident in the fidelity of God and served Jesus' Kingdom cause selflessly. Christian leaders should be empowered to do the same.

As I read the New Testament, the "normal Christian life" is described, above all, as a life of *adventure*. The trust relationship between the Christian and her God was so central, so dynamic, and so pervasive that she was flung, by her faith, into a way of life that was exciting, surprising, and maturity-producing. New Testament church leaders modeled a way of life characterized by bold risk, deep sacrifice, and honest trust.

Sadly, I've observed that most in church leadership today bear little resemblance to their biblical ancestors. *In light of all that God has done for us through the life, death, and resurrection of Jesus we should be among the most courageous human beings to ever walk the planet.* But, in my experience coaching hundreds of pastors over about twenty years, I've found that, as a general rule, we are decidedly *not* courageous.

It seems that few of us remain cognizant of the immensity and universality of God's love for us. If we did, it seems that we'd be willing to live gallant lives that honor him.

To me, this is the key. How easily we forget the empowering love of God. We are so often swayed by our own fears, troubles of life, or the demands and values of the surrounding culture that the truth of what God has said about the Christian diminishes. Often our response is to retreat in fear. But across scripture, God tells his people to "fear not..." So often we hear this as an indictment of our lack of faith. What if we understood "fear not" to be an invitation from a loving Father who is calling us into a life of adventure?

BACK TO BASICS: HOW MINISTRY LEADERS ARE EMPOWERED TO LEAD COURAGEOUSLY

God has promised that he will never leave us or abandon us. According to 2 Peter 1:3, in Jesus, we have all we need to be empowered for impactful ministry. Imagine how you might lead if you truly believed that. If you've forgotten these truths, let me remind you of just a few of the ways that God has promised to be with us and for us.

GOD IS COMPASSIONATE

Consider the amazing provision for we who are God's own. God is called the "Father of compassion" and the "God of all comfort." God stands ready to comfort us in all of life's difficulties. We're not on our own. Not ever. When we attempt to obey the Lord with a valiant ministry initiative and it fails—as often happens—God is poised to bring quick and thorough comfort. [2 Corinthians 1:3-4]

GOD IS TRUSTWORTHY

God affirms the promises he's made to us, declaring them to be absolutely trustworthy and resolute. This means that nothing that God has clearly pledged will go unfulfilled. Further, it is God who causes us to persevere in Christ. God has anointed us, set his seal of ownership upon us, and put his Spirit in our hearts. [2 Corinthians 1:18-22]

GOD DELIGHTS IN HIS CHILDREN

Scripture says that God leads us in a triumphant procession with Jesus. We are a pleasing aroma to God; a fragrance that is potent both for those who are pursuing and those who are rejecting him. This is not something we conjure up. We *are* a delightful fragrance, and we *are* already on display as victors in the most consequential of all ventures. [2 Corinthians 2:14-16]

God Gives Us the Ability to Succeed

We are not only competent as ministers, but our proficiency is not dependent on our own ability, fortitude, or skills. The biblical reality is that *God has given us* the ability to succeed in what we've been called to accomplish. [2 Corinthians 3:4-6]

God Uses All Our Experiences (Good and Bad)

God has promised to use every experience beneficially [Romans 8:28, 2 Corinthians 4:17]. More surprisingly, you and I *are being transformed* into his image with ever-increasing glory, which comes from him! What's crazy is that these promises are not conditioned on our achievement. It is God who has performed spectacularly, and, as a result, *we* receive the splendor of his magnificence. [2 Corinthians 3:18]

God Is Generous

The capacity to trust in Jesus—to actually believe the Gospel and all God has promised—emanates from God's generosity. It is God who made God's light shine in our hearts, giving us the knowledge of God's glory displayed in the face of Christ. [2 Corinthians 4:6]

God Will Complete His Good Work in You

Because of this, you and I are safe and secure as we navigate the events of our lives, encounter its many challenges, and face dangers of all kinds. God started this thing within you, and God has pledged to finish it successfully. [Philippians 1:6]

GOD MAKES ALL THINGS NEW

The Bible states that we who are in Christ are new. New in every way. [Revelation 21:5] I come from a long line of self-made, hard-working types. In my experience, ministry is deeply satisfying as long as there's clarity about God's direction, plenty to do, and some sense that I'm progressing. Take away any of those signposts and I can become bewildered. Fast. Then, I naturally double down on whatever it is that I'm doing, even if it results in fruitless toil.

But, being a new creation in Christ, I've experienced grace to break the generational pattern, pause, and trust God's Spirit to guide me in a new way forward. I'm learning that even my willingness to climb off the merry-go-round of useless effort is evidence of being new. Trusting God can be taxing for high responsibility DIY types, and facile for one whose identity is secure in Christ.

CONCLUSION

I've experienced many setbacks and failures in ministry. I've experienced heart-wrenching times in life, and I'm sure you have too. *But* you and I can have absolute confidence that these experiences haven't disqualified us from ministry. In fact, You and I are *bound for glory.* There can be no other outcome for our lives. No matter what happens here, our mortal existence will be subsumed by a spectacular life reserved in Heaven for us. [2 Corinthians 5:1-4, 1 Peter 1:4]

What I *know* is that the Father wants leaders to be courageous and for churches to thrive even more than we want them to. God, across the centuries, has been faithful to succor, strengthen, rescue, and prosper the intrepid obedience of women and men willing to trust the Lord and align themselves with Kingdom purposes. God delights to be our all-in-all [Psalm 46:1], to watch over us with care [2 Chronicles 16:9], and to remain closer to us than we can comprehend. [Matthew 23:37] If God is with us, who can be against us?

Ultimately, our future is secure. As a result, we can live and lead with courage.

Are you ready?

How to Read This Book

This book is broken up into three parts. In the first section, "The Heart of the Matter" we will explore the path toward how and why a leader *can*, and *should*, embrace courage. This step is not easy. I will invite you to dig deep, go first, and live all-in with your whole heart. Often leaders are thought to be rather impenetrable and stoic. In fact, I believe that *vulnerability of heart* is central to courage.

In part two, "The Condition of the Church," I will explain in more detail the problem within church cultures as I see it. As I've stated already, I believe the Church has embraced America's culture of cowardice and in the process has become ineffective, failing to be salt and light to society at large. This is a hard truth and one that can't be sugar coated. I write plainly in order to get at the heart of the matter as I see it. Some may experience this section as unnecessarily harsh. I'm willing to risk being misunderstood for the sake of clarity. I am not so much angry at the state of church leadership, but sad. I know that church leaders can do something about it! When we go to the doctor for a physical ailment, we need a clear, accurate diagnosis for treatment to begin. Before we're able to step into what leadership courage *is*, we must define what it is *not*. Once the sickness our leadership culture has been identified, a remedy can be considered.

In part three, "Leadership Courage," we will examine what leadership courage looks like in practice, and how to continue in the fight to build a healthier, vision-focused, God honoring culture in your ministry teams. In this section you will discover that this kind of leadership is less about skill and more about the energy and resolve a leader brings to life. We will explore how the leader's *presence* is a catalyst for cultural change over time. If our churches and organizations are going to change for the better, the change must start with our leaders. Standing resolute amidst a culture of fear and cowardice is not easy. It requires resolve, resilience, and stamina – all qualities that God is faithful to grow in you when you step up to the challenge.

A KEY INFLUENCE BEHIND LEADERSHIP COURAGE

I am deeply indebted to Edwin Friedman's seminal work: *A Failure of Nerve*, which has inspired much of the thought behind what you'll read in the pages that follow. As Friedman described the condition of *chronic anxiety* that he argues has overtaken American culture, I was powerfully struck by how greatly his descriptions applied to the Church in North America.

Leadership Courage attempts to illustrate Friedman's principles in the life of Jesus and make direct application to pastors serving in North American churches today.

PART ONE

THE HEART OF THE MATTER

CHAPTER 1

The *Heart* to Lead – Living Courageously

The American church has a courage problem, what Edwin Freidman would call a "failure of nerve." As American culture is changing, fewer people are willing to tolerate the pain of change, and the Church has unfortunately followed suit. In Part Two I will demonstrate ways in which lack of courage in Christian leadership shows itself, and the effects it has.

I suggest *courage is integral to leadership*. The link between the two is inseparable. To attempt to lead anyone, without employing courage, will undermine the possibility of the enterprise you hope to lead others in.

Management is another bird entirely. A manager does not a leader make. I hold an advanced management degree. In graduate school we practiced sophisticated problem-solving techniques. We became proficient using multi-faceted analytic tools such as market, cultural, financial, logistical, and competitive analysis. Most importantly, we developed our abilities at strategic reasoning and planning. In no way is my objective to denigrate management or management education. Yet, leadership is an altogether different matter.

See, *leadership is the visible employment of courage in a way that changes people*: their thinking, behavior, and the impacts of those changes.

What is courage? A friend and mentor defines courage this way: *"Courage is not the absence of fear. Courage is moving forward in the face of fear."* So, what is it that moves one forward in the face of fear? The answer, I think, can be found in the etymology of the word itself.

Our English word, "courage" comes from the French *cor*, which means "heart." Courage literally can mean "with heart." To live courageously is to live with your whole heart.

Your whole heart is engaged.

Your whole heart is invested.

Your whole heart is at stake.

Your whole heart is exposed.

Your whole heart is vulnerable.

What makes this wholehearted living so elusive is that we've all had our hearts hurt. You cannot live, be in relationships, or love without having your heart broken, rejected, or crushed. Since you're not stupid, you learn from each heartbreaking experience not to play so fast and loose with that heart of yours. You've learned to be cautious, protective, and watchful. Once, you lived with your heart in your hand. You put it out there where someone could embrace it as a marvelous, generous, precious gift. Sooner or later it was rejected, repelled, repulsed. That hurt. A lot.

And, since you're no fool, you made sure not to make that mistake again. So, you pulled your heart back. You weren't quite so willing to give your heart away. A person would need to prove himself before you'd loosen your grip on your heart. And, at the first sign of trouble, you'd retrieve it fast!

Then, sometime later, an opportunity presented itself. Possibly, a new venture, a business idea, a ministry, a job, a relationship, or a project. You were skeptical at first, but the idea grew on you. As it did, you became more and more passionate. You began to see yourself *in* it. You decided you could actually see this working out. As you gave yourself to this possibility other priorities fell aside. You invested more deeply. Past the point of "no return."

Then, somehow, in some way you hadn't anticipated, the bottom fell out. Hard and harsh words may have been spoken.

Again, you and your wounded heart retreated from this "folly"—and any future follies as well. From that point forward, you decided you'd be playing your cards a little closer to the vest. What a fool you were to risk like that! What an idiot to trust so indiscriminately!

With each experience, you withdrew your heart to a place less vulnerable, further from other people. Now, you'll be less susceptible to other peoples' whims and vacillations. At the same time, your heart retreated a little farther from your dreams. Closer to your chest.

Eventually, you took that heart of yours and stuffed it back inside your rib cage. Back where you decided it should've been all along. Safe, unexposed, invulnerable, and impenetrable. Like everyone else.

Well… most everyone else.

In AD 185, St. Irenaeus of Lyons in his theologically important treatise *Against Heresies*, is said to have written: *"Man fully alive is the glory of God."* When you take your heart out of your chest and extend it at your arm's full length to those you have affection for, are you not becoming more fully alive? When you put your heart in play, at stake, at risk for some great, worthwhile endeavor, do you not become more fully alive in the process?

A human fully alive is the glory of God.

My introduction to living "all-in" came painfully. Annie and I moved from Indiana to California so that I could attend seminary, join the staff of an exciting church, and pivot from the investment business I'd launched years before for exactly this purpose. I'd experienced the call of God to full-time ministry but had been waiting for God's indication that it was finally time to do it. This was that time.

For the next three years, I navigated a ninety-minute commute, a full academic load as a Masters of Divinity student, ran the investment advisory business for more than 500 clients, and served our church as it mushroomed from 550 to 1,100 on Sundays.

Simultaneously, our six kids entered adolescence as mystifying transformations took over their hormones, personalities, ethics, commitments, and emotions. It was as if alien beings had body-snatched my children. Other than their names and appearance, they bore little resemblance to the children we'd labored so diligently to raise.

I found the changes in my children baffling, befuddling. Incomprehensible. Initial attempts to parent them in this perplexing teen-age world seemed only to drive them further away and to fortify their disdain for me, my values, and counsel. Not knowing what to do, I buried my heart behind my sternum, withdrawing from the confusing cacophony of my kids' adolescence. Instead of leaping unflinchingly into the familial chaos, I poured my energy into work, school, and ministry. Each provided a comforting respite from the mayhem at home, the opportunity to be in control, and the vocal admiration for all I seemed to accomplish.

Late in the night of my seminary graduation a Sheriff called to inform me they'd arrested my son for drug possession. In the car ride home, angry words turned violent, and I landed in the ER for stitches over my eye. We got home just in time for me to shower, change, and race off to church where I was responsible for that morning's Father's Day breakfast.

Defeated and bewildered, I returned to therapy, embarked on a profoundly painful and important character development process, and came face-to-face with what I call "the four horsemen of the apocalypse:" looking good, feeling good, being right, and being in control.

My commitment to the "horsemen" kept me on the sidelines of my own life—like a scientist with clipboard and lab coat—studying the perplexing vicissitudes in my teens but unwilling to step onto the field of play until I knew what to do.

The trouble is *I could never figure out what to do*. Afraid of doing it wrong, of making matters worse I stood frozen on the sidelines of my children's adolescent distress. Years later, while participating in a powerful character-development workshop, I came to realize how I'd lived this season of my life. My heart was lanced. God allowed me to drink deeply from the cup of my children's suffering due to my neglect. This process lasted for months. I was blessed with skilled coaches, like Jean Marie

Jobs, who helped me fix my eyes on the carnage I'd wrought in my family and my cunning devotion to the "four horsemen." It was intensely awful, wonderful work.

In the process, my heart awoke. I began to trust God instead of my strategies to make life manageable. Surrendering my fears to the Lord Jesus, I started to employ my heart again in life, in ministry, and in my relationships. As I did, I began to discover much of what I'm trying to communicate in this book.

In the years since, I've come to realize that because God is absolutely sovereign, nothing is "wrong" with my life. In fact, *I have exactly the life I'm supposed to have.* And, I've learned that my often disorderly, untidy life needs me. More precisely, it needs Jesus. Jesus is present when I bring all of me. Dozens of times since then I've faced situations for which I had no solution. Each time, I've done my best to trust God and leap. And, God has always been there, in the midst of the difficulty, confusion, and pain.

You may be wondering what this story has to do with Christian leadership. Leading well takes risking vulnerability, and being "all in" even when you don't know what comes next. My hope as I've begun leading with my whole heart invested, is that I'm inspiring others to join me. That's leadership.

When we are fully at stake with our eyes wide open, and yet we are still "all in," we invite others in, as well. In fact, when our hearts are fully engaged, we exude an almost irresistible magnetism that pulls others to get in with us. We, and those we inspire, become fully alive.

The glory of God.

The Apostle Paul wrote to the Christ-followers in the commercial and cultural center known as Corinth: "We have spoken freely to you, Corinthians, and opened wide our hearts to you. We are not withholding our affection from you, but you are withholding yours from us. As a fair exchange—I speak as to my children—open wide your hearts also." [2 Corinthians 6:11-13]

As in all affairs of the heart, there is risk. To me it seems one question is always: "Who goes first?" Who gets to be *first* to love, to risk, to be vulnerable?

Paul settles the issue for those of us in ministry: *I* get to go first! In doing so, I model the way of love for all those around me. "We have opened wide our hearts to you." Paul says. "We are not withholding our affection from you."

Of how many in Christian leadership could that be said? How generously, how obviously, or how daringly do we love? How careful are we to not withhold our affection from those we lead?

Most pastors would probably say they love their people well, sacrifice for them, work tirelessly, always try to be accessible, etc. Yet, Paul speaks of *his heart* being wide open to them. That's intense.

A heart wide-open! A big, gaping opening that can be exploited, disappointed, rejected, maligned. And, this is not just for the young, wide-eyed church planters who haven't yet taught themselves to distrust their congregations and to bury their affections behind a mask of professional, religious propriety.

It applies to *you*: the veteran of betrayals, abuses, attacks, and back-stabbings… by many who you'll no doubt find in Heaven. To you, who've been around the block a few times, Paul intones: "We've not withheld our affection."

Heck, how challenging has it been to keep your heart wide open to your spouse? What struggles have you encountered to not withhold your affection from your own husband or wife? How stingy are you with your heart these days?

Francis Frangipane asks in *The Three Battlegrounds*: "Is your love growing and becoming softer, brighter, more daring, and more visible? Or is it becoming more discriminating, more calculating, less vulnerable and less available? This is a very important issue, for your Christianity is only as real as your love is. A measurable decrease in your ability to love is evidence that a stronghold of cold love is developing within you."

Paul, with all that was at stake in Corinth, shepherded his heart so that it remained wide open and was not withheld from them. So rigorously and generously did he give his heart to them that he was able to call them to reciprocate—his *leverage* coming from his having gone first!

He called them to a "fair exchange" of affections.

I wonder if, on those occasions when I have been stunned by the absence of affection I've encountered, it could actually have represented a "fair exchange" of the hiddenness of heart and the stinginess of affection that I'd sown into the relationship. I too have trained myself to keep my heart carefully cloistered where it can't be hurt—much. Yet, this protection comes at a great price.

As humans, let alone Christ-followers, we were made for love. Made to love, we are built to access and share affection readily, easily, and generously, like little kids do. Remember?

Living with and among imperfect human beings, I've been hurt and I've seen others hurt over the years. In the movies and on TV we see characters that give the appearance of being deeply satisfied, fully alive, and relationally connected without the risk of hurt and heartache that love requires. Smooth operators. Cool customers.

Cold lovers?

I once taught myself to be in life that way. Denying what I was, and what I was made for until Christ captured my heart and taught me another way: a risky way, a vulnerable, dangerous way. Since then, there's been an accordion-like opening and closing, expanding and compressing of the affections my heart was meant to exude.

For the past two decades I've been intentionally entering the rigor to open my heart wide and to war against the regular impulses to withhold my affection from those I influence. Imperfectly and purposefully, I'm giving myself to this dangerous and delightful way of life. As I do, I'm calling others to engage in a "fair exchange" of affection.

What might God do among those you lead, if you were to surrender your many efforts to keep your heart safe? What if you were to trust God and open your heart wide to those you lead? Just know that when you open your heart to those you lead, there is a cost, but it is well worth it.

FOR PERSONAL REFLECTION:

The Apostle Paul writes: "We have spoken freely to you, Corinthians, and opened wide our hearts to you. We are not withholding our affection from you…"

- On a scale of 1% – 100% how open (i.e. vulnerable) is your heart to those closest to you? If 100% is as open as your heart could be, how open is your heart to your spouse? Your children? Your boss? Your subordinates?

- Compared to five years ago, is your heart generally more, or less, accessible to others?

- Of the people you admire, who lives with the greatest vulnerability-of-heart?

- What are three impacts of that way of life on those they influence?

- If you could choose, how open would you *want* your heart to be?

FOR GROUP DISCUSSION:

In *The Three Battlegrounds*, Francis Frangipane asks: "Is your love growing and becoming softer, brighter, more daring, and more visible? Or is it becoming more discriminating, more calculating, less vulnerable and less available?"

- In pairs, give each other honest feedback about the degree to which your partner's love is either growing or becoming less available.

- With whom does this person struggle most to love visibly and daringly?

- Brainstorm three specific ways your love could become "softer, brighter, more daring, and more visible."

- As a team, organization, or group is your collective love becoming more or less discriminating, calculating, vulnerable, and available?
- What "slope" (upward *or* downward) would you give the trajectory of your love for one another over the past two to three years?

CHAPTER 2

The Price of Love

To review, living with heart and vulnerability requires courage. Some would argue that living with your heart fully engaged, fully invested, and fully in play is costly, reckless, and dangerous. I agree. To live with your heart withheld is also costly.

There's no living without paying prices. Give your heart; there are prices. Hide your heart from your own life and *other* prices are exacted.

So, let's examine prices that living with heart requires. Just to be clear about it.

Whenever *you care* about anyone and anything, you invest some of yourself. The more deeply you care, the more of yourself you invest. Initially, maybe all you invest are thoughts and ideas about what could be, what a ministry or business endeavor could mean, and what it could become.

Before long, you begin to entertain how you might be affected. How you might contribute. You consider what good could come through it and how you could benefit if it succeeds. As you do, you give yourself permission to see the possibility of what this could lead to or what it could become.

As hearts are wont to do, your heart gets gripped. Not only do you see this as preferable, you begin to *love* what this might become. Now wanting it, you give yourself to it, a bit at a time. Giving more of yourself as you go. More of your time, your focus, your attention. As you pour yourself into having it happen you are changed. Some of what used to hold your attention no longer does.

People notice.

No longer repressing your enthusiasm, you invite others in with you. Some people back away. They want nothing to do with your stupid dream.

Most are satisfied to stay on the sideline. Amused, they watch to see whether your dreams will be dashed or fulfilled. They wait to see if it's safe to join you.

And, a few *are* enrolled. They choose to leap with you into the possibility of what could be. As they do, your relationships change. The stakes are now higher. "If this thing goes south," you catch yourself thinking. "A lot of people could get hurt." "And, if we succeed…"

Momentum seems to come from everywhere. Connections appear in surprising ways. Provision arrives unexpectedly. It's like there's a wind at your back, propelling you forward. You *feel* alive. Energized. Hopeful. Life seems to open up before you. It expands.

At the same time, loved-ones caution you not to get in too deep. Remember the movie *Rudy?* It's the story of a young man's ambition to leave the steel mill that employs his relatives and attend college at Notre Dame and play football there. The problem is, Rudy has neither the grades not the athletic prowess to be a candidate for either. There's a scene at the bus station when Rudy's decision is confronted by his father. His dad counsels: "Chasing a stupid dream causes you and everyone around you nothing but heartache."

You've heard the message too: Don't go too far. Don't move so fast. What about the risks? What if this doesn't work? Don't you care about *us*? All along the way, with your heart engaged, you are paying prices. You set aside the predictable, the familiar, and the safe. You wade into murky waters. So much is unknown, untested, and uncertain.

Disappointments come, as they must. Setbacks catch you off-guard. Betrayals stun you. Backlash comes from unexpected sources. Supporters withdraw. Criticisms that began as a whisper grow in ferocity. You feel alone.

And, each time, your hopeful heart is nicked. Lanced. Pierced. Wounded. You want to pull back, disinvest, protect yourself, be reasonable, find balance, and cut your losses. Most of all, you want to rescue your heart from the hurt.

Remember C.S. Lewis' quote about love from the introduction? It bears repeating. He writes, "Love anything and your heart will certainly be wrung and possibly be broken. If you want to make sure of keeping it intact, you must give your heart to no one…"

To live and lead with courage is to love so much that your heart is vulnerable to being "wrung and possibly broken." Yet, when your heart *is* wrung or broken, you can choose to keep it engaged. Silencing your survival instincts, trusting God to heal and strengthen your heart, you keep giving yourself—fully—to your life.

This is no small matter. If it were, the world would be full of powerfully courageous leaders. Imagine if the Church—even your church—was a gathering place, an equipping place, and a sending place for leaders like this.

To summarize, I believe the first key to courageous leadership is choosing to live all-in, with your whole heart. This requires a vulnerability that's easy to see in the life of Jesus and the Apostle Paul. This degree of whole-heartedness is rare in the lives of most American clergy. The second key to courageous leadership is taking responsibility *for yourself*, while simultaneously remaining responsible *to* others. There's a big difference.

THE RESPONSIBILITY RIDDLE

I'd like to pose a scenario to illustrate the peculiar relationship many leaders have with responsibility. I'm sitting across from a pastor asking a series of questions meant to get to the heart of the topic.

Question: Pastor, who is responsible for your spiritual maturity and vitality?

Answer: I am, of course!

Ok, fine. Now answer this...

Question: Pastor, who is responsible for the spiritual maturity and vitality of your congregation?

Answer: Again, I am!

Question: Really? Are you sure?

If *you* are responsible for your congregation's spiritual maturity, what are *they* responsible for?

My purpose in going through this hypothetical conversation is meant to make a point: There's a troubling trend in the Church these days. We, in ministry, see the evidence of it all the time. It can be found in a complaint. More often than not, the complaint sounds something like this: "I'm just not getting fed here," "I don't experience the presence of God here," or "The worship no longer ministers to me."

And then, off they go, out the door, on to another church, or maybe to no church at all. The thinking, both of the pastor and the complaining congregants flows from the same fallacy: that the pastor, the church, and the elders are somehow responsible for the spiritual condition of those they serve.

Thinking like this, it's no wonder the Church is diapered in spiritual infancy.

So, who is responsible for your spiritual maturity and vitality? You are. Only you. The responsibility riddle can be solved in this important, seldom recognized distinction: Your pastor is responsible to you, but is not responsible for you.

Think about it. A pastor is responsible to the congregation to model mature faith in action, to proclaim God's Word faithfully, to represent Christ ethically. Each believer is responsible for what they do with the Word of God: both the preached Word and the Word that sits in their lap, is available on their phone, on the bookshelf, or on the coffee table gathering dust.

Are you responsible for your spouse's happiness? Of course not! How could you be?

If your spouse has handed you "the keys" to their emotional well-being, please give them back! Now.

When you notice that someone has tried to make you responsible for whatever it is that God has made *them* responsible for—their attitudes, their feelings, their behavior, their "stress," their decisions, their depression, their optimism—invite them to embrace this reality: you may have a responsibility *to* them, but you can never be responsible *for* them.

Do I have a responsibility to Annie, my wife? Absolutely! I am responsible to keep my promises to her. I've promised to value her above every breathing human being. I've promised to honor her whether she deserves it or not. I've promised to pray for her. I've promised to champion her toward all God's called her to be. I've promised to be faithful both sexually and emotionally. I've promised to walk with God and to submit my life to Jesus and his Word. I promised to treat her better than she deserves. But, she is responsible for herself. Completely.

When our kids were small and unable to take responsibility for themselves, as parents we bore the responsibility for them. When our pre-teen had a friend over and they snuck out at night and set fire to a porta-potty, we were legally responsible because they were minors. They were under our supervision. Now that he's an adult, it would be foolish for Annie and me to take responsibility for his decisions. In fact, it would be irresponsible of us to do so. To take responsibility for another adult is a violation of his or her autonomy. It is an invasion of their sovereignty. I believe it also represents a kind of abuse. Yes, abuse.

When you are with an otherwise capable adult as if they were incapable of adult choices and unable to bear the adult consequences for those choices, there is an impact—a "fruit" that is produced. This happens whenever you persuade another to live irresponsibly.

The distinction of being *responsible to* vs. *responsible for* is central for any of us in leadership. There's actually great freedom when you are clear about this distinction, and lead in such a way that those you influence are clear about it too. To stand in life responsible to others and responsible for your own emotional being and destiny may call for courage you've not been willing to summon, up 'till now.

It's time to call it up!

FOR PERSONAL REFLECTION:

Consider the distinction between being *responsible to* vs being *responsible for* those in your life.

- In which two relationships have you most egregiously violated this principle?
- In what ways have you made yourself *responsible for* an otherwise capable adult?
- How has this posture sown mischief into the relationship?
- What three benefits have you received (feeling important, powerful, valuable, being admired) as a result of your over-functioning in this way?
- What are four prices that have been paid by those you've taken responsibility for?
- How has their impact, development, maturity been compromised?
- If you were to stand *responsible to* this person, rather than *responsible for* them, what, in you, would have to change?

FOR GROUP DISCUSSION:

Consider the ways in which your organization's leadership takes *responsibility for* those they lead.

- Collaborate to identify ten ways your organization's leadership practices and is postured as if they are *responsible for* the choices of those they lead.
- In what specific ways does this over-functioning burden and exhaust the leadership?
- Discuss how the over-functioning contributes to those you lead failing to stand responsible for their own attitudes, actions, and impact.

- To begin to declare a new relationship to responsibility, what three important communication events need to be created by your leadership team?

- Wrestle together until you can agree on language that will support these communications.

- What safeguards can you attempt to keep the leadership from falling back into a *"responsible for"* posture with your organization?

PART TWO

THE CONDITION OF THE CHURCH

CHAPTER 3

A Culture of Cowardice

It is important to open with this disclaimer: I love the Church. *And,* I'm concerned for her. I was born in 1955, a time when, for many, the Church in North America was far more consequential than it is today. Then as now, the Church *is* Jesus' bride. The object of God's affection. Since the Day of Pentecost, God has chosen to be revealed to humanity in and through the Church. Yes, the heavens declare the glory of God

[Psalm 19:1] *and* God has chosen to proclaim his invitation through people. [Romans 10:14-15]

As you read what follows, you might conclude that I'm angry with the Church. Or that I'm frustrated. Or that I have an ax to grind because I've been hurt by someone in Church leadership whose failure injured me. No. As much as I know my own heart and motivations, my primary emotion is heartbreak, not anger. I love Jesus' bride and I'm concerned for her future. You see, the Church is to be God's redemptive gift to salt and light the communities where God has placed it.

By "salt" I mean that capacity to *spice up* the experience of living in God; and all humans are living in God whether they acknowledge or deny that reality. Historically, salt's seasoning effect was experienced as good. In addition to seasoning all it touches, salt *preserves*. Salt slows decay. In the arid Middle East at the time of Christ, salt kept meat from rotting. It was essential to survival. Everybody understood this.

"Light" illuminates. Light can point the way like a car's headlights serve those driving, warn of danger the way a lighthouse does, and enable us to see when vision would otherwise be impossible. Light allows us to make helpful distinctions in thousands of beneficial ways that keep us from harm, make sense of our surroundings, to read, to learn, and to respond advantageously. Without it, society is confined to grope in darkness, suffering needlessly, sorrowing greatly.

When churches fail to be salt and light in our communities, our congregations suffer, but the unchurched around us suffer much more.

Who are the exemplars of courage in society today? Often, it's pop-culture icons or sports stars with little evidence of moral fiber. It seems to me that the courageous have become an endangered species in society and in the Church.

Think about it.

Wikipedia defines an endangered species as a population *"at risk of becoming extinct, because it is either few in numbers or threatened by changing environmental or predation parameters."* Can you see that these conditions are true of the Church today? We're left with what I call a "culture of cowardice."

In the early 1990's, Dr. Edwin Friedman described America as "a seatbelt society." He noted that our culture had oriented itself more toward safety than adventure. In *A Failure of Nerve* he notes that America has become so chronically anxious that our society has gone into an emotional regression that is toxic to courageous, well-defined leadership.

One effect of societal anxiety is a reduced pain threshold. The result: we value comfort over the rewards of facing and surmounting challenges.

A culture like this has no stamina in the face of difficulty and crisis.

How like the contemporary Church this is. In our commitment to "being nice" we have prioritized togetherness over making a difference. In our desire to *feel* good we bury our heads in the proverbial sand while the culture around us sprints toward its destruction. According to Friedman, in environments like this, dissent is discouraged, feelings take precedence over ideas, peace over progress, comfort over anything new, and cloistered virtues over adventure.

The pressure within church for togetherness smothers bold, daring, world-changing action—like we see in the Book of Acts—and those who are courageous enough to engage it. I'm not one to sentimentalize the "early church." The early church had its own problems, and we have ours. Scripture describes a Church that was strong, courageous, bold, and risk-taking. Do you see this kind of fervor in the average church-goer today? What has emerged is a church culture that is so nice, and so fixated on empathy that it organizes itself around the most immature, most dependent, most dysfunctional members.

Who has hijacked the agenda in most of America's churches? In my experience working with hundreds of church leaders from across the denominational spectrum, I've found that the least courageous, least responsible, and least emotionally and spiritually mature are often the ones who have taken most churches captive.

ATTRIBUTES OF COURAGEOUS LEADERSHIP

Courageous leadership is decisive

The Latin root of decisive means "to cut." However, in church it is rarely nice to cut anything away, to cut anything off, or to cut anything out—even when it's a toxic presence that, like a parasite, survives by sucking the life out of those who are healthier. To lead with heart is to stand for what's best for the church, simply because it is best—even when that stand is unpopular. Even when it provokes opposition from stakeholders in the Church.

Courageous leadership is *clear*

A courageous leader is unapologetically clear about who she is, the difference she is committed to make in the world, and her values and priorities. *The clearer you are as a leader, the clearer people around you become.*

And, therein lies the problem. As pastors, we don't always like what that clarity reveals. As you become increasingly clear as a leader, more people will decide they're not willing to go where you're headed. Stay foggy and many will stay with you, wandering around in impotent ambiguity.

Courageous leadership is *disruptive*

Courageous leaders routinely disrupt dysfunction. They regularly challenge their own preference for comfort—and that of those they lead.

Mature leaders understand that their leadership is crisis-inducing.

Let me repeat that: *healthy leadership is crisis-inducing.*

Friedman notes that crises are normative in leaders' lives. These crises come from two sources: those that just arise, imposed on the leader from forces outside that leader's control *and* crises that are initiated simply by the leader doing exactly what he or she should be doing. As you study Jesus' leadership, particularly with his disciples, you'll be stunned how frequently he invokes adversity for those closest to him. Yet, how reluctant is anyone in church leadership to lead in a way that *invites a crisis* for long-standing church members?

As a leadership coach and consultant to pastors, my life's work is to champion Christian influencers *to find their hearts and to fully re-engage them* in the great, important struggle to stir the Church from her slumber. There is no altogether "nice" way to do this.

Just five verses into his story, Jonah is sound asleep below deck, aboard a ship imperiled by a brutal storm. The terrified captain races below, stunned to find Jonah asleep in so important a moment. He wakes Jonah demanding: *"How can you sleep? Get up and call on your God! Maybe he will take notice of us, and we will not perish."* [Jonah 1:6] Get this: it was not a follower of Yahweh who stirred Jonah from slumber— calling him to take action with God lest the community they'd become be plunged to ruin.

Look around you. Isn't the community outside your church caught in a destructive tempest? In my observation, an ethical, spiritual, economic, and relational hurricane is threatening to destroy the fabric of American society. This same storm is buffeting the Christian faith and driving it to the very edges of the culture.

To awaken the Church, her leaders must first rouse *themselves*. Then, embracing the opportunity provided by this life, they can stand clearly, decisively, and disruptively to awaken their churches to enter the glorious and dangerous fight for the redemption of the unchurched near them.

What else would a courageous Christian do?

A CULTURE OF COWARDICE PRIORITIZES COMFORT

Another feature of a culture of cowardice is that it is toxic to courageous, well-differentiated leadership. So acute is the culture's abhorrence of discomfort, it knee-jerks its way from one perceived threat to another, clamoring for instantaneous relief from ministers who are pulled in all directions at once. While a pastor may have begun serving a church with a clear sense of mission, in short order that mission is subordinated by the demand that the emergency of the moment be averted with all haste.

Instead of challenging the congregation to maturity and to take important new ground in strengthening their intimacy with, and dependence on the Lord Jesus, ministers become consumed with smoothing out the never-ending ruffled feathers of the flock.

Caretaking is not leadership.

A constituency that is developmentally infantilized requires that a clergyperson do little more than immerse one's finger in the mouth, stick it up in the breeze, and move in the path of least resistance. This, according to Friedman, will be to accommodate the low frustration tolerance of the developmentally regressed. To do this, all pastors need is to answer their emails or phone.

A leader who remains resolute in pursuit of a cause greater than the good feelings of the congregation—for example, the maturation of the disciples and the mobilization of the membership for ministry to those outside—is seen as heartless, unresponsive, deaf to the cries of the downtrodden, and out of touch with the "real people" within. Emotionally and spiritually emaciated church members have no stomach for a *real* leader...like Christ.

IF JESUS WAS A MEMBER OF A TYPICAL AMERICAN CHURCH

To a member of a beleaguered minority Jesus declared: "You have no idea what you're worshipping!" [John 4:22] Embarrassed by Jesus' insensitivity, the church might howl: "How cruel, abusive, and bigoted! Our all-loving Heavenly Father is nothing like that!"

To a fellow Jesus invites to follow him, he says: "Let the dead bury their dead" when someone asks permission to first attend his father's funeral. [Luke 9:60] To this, the church would smugly declare: "How unfeeling, cold, and heartless! A merciful God would never say that!"

When Jesus comes upon the merchants in the temple, he goes nuts: vandalizing their property, shooing the animals away, and misappropriating their funds. [John 2:15] Surely, the church of today would get a restraining order against Jesus—after his involuntary psychiatric hold had expired. "God is a God of order, not chaos," they'd likely intone.

In short, Jesus is revealed in scripture as clear, decisive, and disruptive.

You might think Him a study in contrasts. On the one hand, he is compassionate to the adulteress. On the other, he appears hair-triggered to undermine the religious hypocrisy of his day. No doubt he would be branded a troublemaker in most American churches today.

Think about your current church or system. Imagine if a leader this clear, this resolute, and this determined were influential. What if that leader operated *outside* the established leadership hierarchy? What if this person's no-nonsense approach began to enjoy a following from many outside the institutional mainstream?

Jesus was resolute in his commitment to model, bring, and defend the Kingdom of his Father. Period.

Often, Christian leaders fail to reflect Jesus' resolute commitment, but we are tasked in large part with challenging our congregations to change. The question is, will we take up that challenge?

FOR PERSONAL REFLECTION:

Edwin Friedman observed that the United States had become so chronically anxious that our society had gone into an emotional regression that is toxic to courageous, well-defined leadership. One effect of this, he pointed out, is a reduced pain threshold.

- In what ways has your pain threshold been reduced over the past decade?
- What dreams have you surrendered in favor of comfort and predictability?
- What are the two most difficult conversations you've avoided having, and with whom?
- What prices does your relationship pay because of your cowardice?
- What would you have to surrender in order to devote yourself afresh to two of the dreams you've released?

FOR GROUP DISCUSSION:

The author claims that in most churches the agenda has been "hijacked" by the least courageous, least responsible, and least emotionally and spiritually mature.

- To what degree is this dynamic operating in your organization? In what three zones are the least mature exercising outsized influence?
- How has the influence of the less mature weakened resolve in your organization?
- How has your organization, over the last decade or two, regressed in its willingness to endure pain in pursuit of greater accomplishments?

- Work together to identify four examples of the organization buckling under pressure from the less mature to abandon a potentially worthwhile endeavor.

- What would it require of senior leadership to wrestle the "keys" to your organization back from those who are less tolerant of pain and difficulty?

Firmly Owned:
Organization not Disorganization

CHAPTER 4

The Challenge of Change

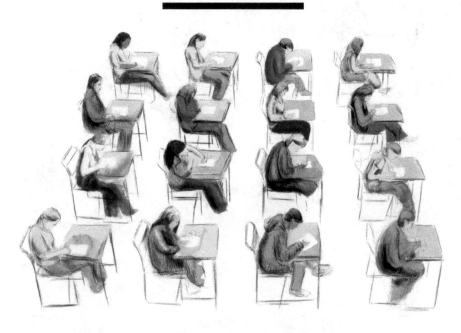

Regardless of your church polity, my observation is that no one has as great an opportunity to influence the culture and values of a local church than the senior minister. That is why I've dedicated my life to standing with and strengthening *them*.

You who speak from the pulpit determine what your congregants talk about. To the degree that you choose your title, topic, or text when you preach, you inject that into the congregational conversation that takes place in the cars and restaurants and kitchens of those who hear. Now, you don't get to determine *what they say* about your topic, but you *do* get to decide what that topic is.

Think about it.

How consistently does your preaching provoke people to think? Do your sermons unsettle the status quo? To what degree do your messages undermine mediocrity wherever it influences your congregation? Are you challenging your people to change?

If not, why not?

Re-read the Gospels and focus on the words printed in red. Notice how often Jesus did exactly that. Jesus stood as an interruption to everything that came between his hearers and the Kingdom of God. Jesus constantly provoked, unsettled, undermined, and challenged those he was with.

Jesus loved them enough to affront and assail that which would do them harm—even when they cherished it as good, nice, or comfortable. He loved the rich young ruler enough to spell out exactly what it would take for him to inherit eternal life. [Mark 10:21] Love motivated Jesus to challenge him. Love—not for himself, his comfort, or reputation—but love for the other moved Christ to risk an offense.

I assert that it is love that motivates pastors to *retreat* from challenging, offending, and opposing the mediocrity your parishioners hold as true. By mediocrity I mean those who merely attend church services, and perhaps belong to Christian organizations but are not personally experiencing life transformation or sacrificing much of anything that would put their personal comfort at risk. Trouble is, it is not love *for them* that keeps you from goring their sacred cows of compromise.

You don't want the push back. You say to yourself, there's no point in stirring up a hornet's nest. You're already on thin ice with several stakeholders in the church. No need to rock the boat. You're already tired enough. Besides, they've made you pay when your preaching got too personal a while back.

Thank God that Jesus didn't fear offending the woman at the well, because it is likely that she and her whole village would have perished had he played it safe. What if Jesus chose to quench his zeal [Psalm 69:9, John 2:17] rather than go after the powerful and popular merchants in the temple?

Courageous leadership is leadership with heart. With *your* heart fully exposed, fully engaged, fully at-stake. There is no virtue in being a jerk. I'm not advocating that you be oppositional just because you can. Nor am I suggesting that you blast away at whoever and whatever bothers you, just to get something off your chest. No, that would be selfish.

To risk your own security, your comfort, and the way others regard you for *their* benefit—that is love. Standing powerfully resolute because of your love for someone else, in the face of ridicule and rejection—this is exactly what Jesus did.

OTHER-FOCUSED LOVE CHALLENGES

Two decades ago, I attended a series of character development trainings. Each was designed to serve both as a crucible and a spotlight—to allow me to see aspects of my character and my impact on others that I was blind to.

Jean Marie Jobs is a powerfully incisive woman who had trained four of my children in this character development work. In the process, she heard first-hand what it was like for them to have me as their dad. I'll summarize it this way: distant, demanding, disconnected, self-consumed, rigid, judgmental, severe, angry, and cold. Then, she facilitated a workshop that Annie attended. She learned of Annie's frustration, disappointment, loneliness, and anguish living with a spouse like me.

For the next five years, Jean Marie served as my coach and trainer. I had never met anyone like her. Her love for my family and for me was palpable, undeniable, and unrelenting, as was her full-court press to challenge my self-consumption. She repeatedly provoked me to consider my true impact on those I love. She consistently undermined my commitment to remain clueless; a strategy I'd employed to stay self-satisfied and undisturbed by the dysfunction inherent in my most important relationships. She interrupted my cherished excuses (too busy, too important, over-committed, doing the best I can) and the beliefs that supported them. She opposed my well-worn practice of hiding from life when I didn't know what to do, and she offended the arrogance of my belief that the way *I* viewed life was "right." Jean Marie unsettled the confidence I'd placed in my self-perceived innocence and virtue.

Up to that time, there were people who loved me and overlooked my childishness, selfishness, and playing small. Others, recoiling at the putrid odor of my self-righteousness would have nothing to do with it or me. Jean Marie was different. She was sickened by the offensiveness of my hypocrisy, yet she loved me steadfastly. It was her love that held me in the cleansing fire she brought.

Oh, that I would love so well!

Changing Lives?

One insight that emerged from my time with Jean Marie is that *pain is necessary for change.*

You and I would prefer to believe that an appropriately reasonable rationale, cloaked in kindness, is all that is needed for humans to embrace the adventure and uncertainty of the unknown. Since the Enlightenment, I suppose, societies have assumed that knowledge of what's better will result in people making the reasoned choice to change. But if we're honest, most people *don't* make reasoned choices, and those people include *us*.

One condition that's welcomed the stagnation common to the church experience of most Christians is that *we who are in leadership have forgotten what business we are in.*

Now, I'm no historian, but my understanding is that the Protestant Reformation occurred within the sweep of the Enlightenment—the Age of Reason—and we've been reasoning with our congregations ever since. Reasoning kindly with them about the truths of the Bible. We've been teaching the Word as if we're in the education business.

The problem is, education, for those of us in ministry, is not an end in itself. An educated church person is not an end either. No more than an elevator is an end. An elevator is a means to the 11th floor. Teaching the Bible is a means to an end. As I asserted in the introduction, the Church is in the life-change business. When someone approaches you with "Nice message, Pastor," is your reply: "Thank you?"

More often than not, when someone approaches me with a similar encouragement, my reply is "Why?" I listen for how the person has been impacted. Then I want to know: "So what?" "How will you live differently?" You see, if my teaching and preaching (and this book, for that matter) does not change the way you live, I have wasted your time and mine.

Pastor, if you are not changing lives in identifiable, maturity-inducing ways, aren't you wasting your time and that of the one who hears you? Multiply this by the 90 or 390 people in your church, then multiply that by the months, years, and decades that you've been educating people whose lives are not radically changing and what do you have?

The Church in North America.

LOVE UNSETTLES US

Which brings me back to pain. Minister, if you are in the life-changing business then you are in the distress-bringing business as well. Many will argue that to bring distress to your congregation is unkind. But it's not. Jean Marie brought me distress, and her insistence to continually provoke my growth was loving. Immensely loving.

The Message renders 2 Corinthians 7:8-9 this way: "I know I distressed you greatly with my letter. Although I felt awful at the time, I don't feel at all bad now that I see how it turned out. The letter upset you, but only for a while. Now I'm glad—not that you were upset, but that you were jarred into turning things around. You let the distress bring you to God, not drive you from him."

Paul wrote to change their lives. He explains that his previous letter was to see if they'd take responsibility for the church. [2 Corinthians. 2:9] Notice that Paul's discourse produced distress and upset. It "jarred" them into turning things around.

Pastor, when was the last time you jarred your people? How long has it been since your preaching provoked such sorrow in your people that it ignited a change-of-life the Bible calls "repentance?"

Would you love your people well enough to provoke them to suffer—unto repentance? In *The Problem of Pain* CS Lewis wrote: "Love is something more stern and splendid than mere kindness. Kindness, merely as such, cares not whether its object becomes good or bad, provided only that it escapes suffering." So consider: do you love your congregation sternly and splendidly, or has it been your aim to ceaselessly rescue them from suffering?

This, I think, is a second condition that's invited the spiritual lethargy that's settled over the Church like the marine layer that engulfs San Francisco Bay.

Our *over-commitment to be kind* has left our people immature and shallow.

Edwin Friedman suggests what Paul modeled: *it is through challenge that we promote responsibility in our people.* To be a leader who will jar your people to maturity you must raise *your* pain threshold.

It follows then that you must also raise *your* threshold for the pain you cause others. This means in part that we are willing to turn on the light to reveal areas of our own lives that we'd rather keep hidden. It also means we lovingly expose others to that same light.

TURN ON THE LIGHT

How is it that when a prominent Christian leader falls, the whole affair is so often shrouded in darkness? The secrecy seems to persist until the police, the media, an offended party, or the victim of the leadership abuse brings it into the light. How often are those illuminations met with skillfully-articulated denials or a minimizing reinterpretation of the offense? Is it just me, or do you see it, too?

Christians are often fond of reciting John 8:32 *"Then you will know the truth, and the truth will set you free"* particularly when the topic is evangelism. The trouble is, our behavior—at very important times and in very important ways—*often covers up the truth.*

The Greek word translated "truth" is *alethia,* meaning "reality," or "what is." Yet, in times of crisis—like when a minister falls in sin—we seem to invest ourselves in elaborate cover-ups. One reason we do, I think, is because the Church has forgotten what business it's in. Remember, ministry leadership is about being in the "people-development business."

Is it any wonder those outside our faith community scratch their heads about us? What are they to think when we froth at the mouth about the "truth" of our Gospel and then behave in ways that endeavor to keep truth hidden? Were the roles reversed, what would you think? How likely would you be to consider their faith claims?

Andy Stanley in *The Next Generation Leader* correctly identifies courage as central to leadership. One of the ways leadership courage expresses itself, he says, is in recognizing and declaring current reality—regardless of how embarrassing or discouraging it is. When a prominent pastor falls, the courageous around him or her will honestly and forthrightly communicate the truth of what has happened. Because being in the people-development business often times means we have to get out of the keep-the-people-comfortable business. Courageous leaders recognize this as a critical character-development opportunity.

A leadership failure is "ground zero" for anchoring the central values that Christ-followers are committed to live. When Paul instructed Timothy: *"Those [elders] who sin are to be rebuked publicly, so that the others may take warning."* [1 Timothy 5:20], he placed the benefit to "the others" above whatever prices the leaders or the fallen elder would experience. And, I invite you to consider that "the others" who are warned are not just those inside the Church.

Yet, for centuries, we in Christendom have routinely swept these humiliations under the rug: the priest is relocated to a new parish, the pastor takes a seminary position, the missionary goes on furlough, and the youth leader enrolls in graduate school. Those close enough to the transgression become collateral damage and often leave the church, and the Faith.

Paul counsels Timothy against favoritism in leading the church and administering discipline when he writes: "I charge you, in the sight of God and Christ Jesus and the elect angels, to keep these instructions without partiality, and to do nothing out of favoritism." [1 Timothy 5:21]. Yet, isn't that what we so often do?

Several years ago, I became aware of an egregious ethical compromise by a nationally visible leader with whom I had worked. When my attempts to influence a correction were uniformly thwarted, I resigned. The public explanation provided by that leader was an example of the positive-sounding pablum of most such announcements. It said nothing.

And, saying nothing, it succeeded in saying one thing clearly: "*What you're being told is not the truth.*"

So, when people close to the situation asked why I resigned, I told them. I shared my errors in judgment, my failures to act on the prompting of the Holy Spirit years before, and my mistakes—the ways I'd contributed to the mess. In addition, I shared, as honestly as I knew, what those in leadership, including this respected national leader, had done.

When we claim to be "children of light" yet switch off the light when what it reveals is unpleasant or uncomely or uncomfortable, are we not strengthening the darkness? Does not the murkiness thicken when the Church fails to stand as light in life? Paul, to the church in Ephesus wrote: "For you were once darkness, but now you are light in the Lord. Live as children of light (for the fruit of the light consists in all goodness, righteousness and truth) and find out what pleases the Lord. We should have nothing to do with fruitless deeds of darkness, but rather expose them.

But everything exposed by the light becomes visible, for it is light that makes everything visible." [Ephesians 5:8-14]

Living within a culture of cowardice, we find it awkward to expose darkness the way Paul instructs. Orienting ourselves around the least mature, our response to a moral failure is to *make it easy for the fallen leader.* We tell ourselves that the "restoration" of the fallen leader is most important. So, we keep the indiscretion secret. We keep it in the dark.

Paul didn't see it that way.

_____

In the business of making mature disciples, courageous leaders will mourn with those who fall *and* warn everyone else, lest we disavow the truth we profess by the way we lead.

Section Two of this book has been my attempt to describe the context in which Christian leaders find themselves today. I've labeled it "a culture of cowardice." You may quibble with a point or two, but it doesn't seem like a stretch to say that the Church in North America today is a far cry from the refreshing, world-changing, dynamo that God's Spirit birthed in the Book of Acts.

Now we turn to a distinctive quality of leadership that I believe is essential in this hour. Without it, the American Church, with American society right behind it, will continue to collapse into that of Western Europe.

FOR PERSONAL REFLECTION:

CS Lewis wrote: "Love is something more stern and splendid than mere kindness. Kindness, merely as such, cares not whether its object becomes good or bad, provided only that it escapes suffering."

- Reflect on your preaching over the last year or two. Review your sermon titles. To what degree has your focus been to alleviate distress in your people, to protect them from suffering?

- To what degree has your focus, instead, been to provoke their maturity in Christ-likeness?

- Consider your responses to difficult or prickly interpersonal challenges over this same season. How would you rate, say on a scale of 1-100, your threshold for experiencing the pain of disappointing people?

- When you started out in ministry was your pain threshold stronger or weaker?

- What has accounted for the change?

- In what ways could you trust God with people's response to your challenges to their immaturity?

FOR GROUP DISCUSSION:

In 2 Corinthians 7 Paul writes: "I know I distressed you greatly with my letter...The letter upset you, but only for a while. Now I'm glad... that you were jarred into turning things around. You let the distress bring you to God..."

- As a leadership team, rate your willingness to "distress" one another in order to produce more God-honoring results.

- Discuss your team's experience of being "jarred into turning things around." What jarred you? How did each of you respond? How were things "turned around" as a result?

- Individually, if you had been able to avoid being distressed 100% of the time over the last decade, what benefits (to your character development, particularly) would you have missed?

- What can you do, as a team, to bring "distress" like Paul did, to those you influence, as a way to point them to God?

- How can you increase your threshold for the pain you cause others?

PART THREE

PRINCIPLES OF LEADERSHIP COURAGE

CHAPTER 5

Presence

How is a pastor, denominational executive, lay leader, elder, or board member to lead when the culture of your organization is shot through with cowardice?

What are the implications for George Barna's "Revolutionaries" who've been so sickened by the self-soothing silliness in churches that, while ministering passionately and creatively for Christ, they've cut themselves off from the local church? And, what of the thousands upon thousands of Christians who, frustrated by the infantile institutionalism and the soft-headed social activism of mainline denominations, have washed their hands of the whole religious mess?

Picture yourself with the New Testament in one hand and Edwin Friedman's *A Failure of Nerve* in the other. What if Jesus, our exemplar, understood Friedman better than Friedman understood himself? What follows are nine characteristics of leadership, modeled by Jesus, that emerge from my understanding of Friedman's seminal work.

One: Courageous leadership is not about skill, technique, or knowledge. It is, most of all, about the *presence* of the leader as he or she moves through life.

In *Generation to Generation*, Friedman gives this definition of a leader: *"A self-defined person with a non-anxious presence."*

In this Chapter we will examine one attribute of courageous leadership: decisive self-definition.

By "self-defined," I mean a person who has a clear sense of her unique calling from God and is living in alignment with that calling. It's not enough to intellectually embrace who you're called to be and the unique difference you've been prepared to make [Ephesians 2:10] if you live *as if* you were someone else. So many, in my estimation, live with a puny, self-consuming purpose like feeling loved, being happy, or feeling good about myself. Please!

Consider Jesus' example. Notice the clarity he embodies as he moves through his relationships, through his world. At age twelve, he's in the temple, discussing the Law with the priests. Once his parents find him, his mother demands an explanation for his behavior. Jesus replies with a question: "Didn't you know that I must be about my father's business?" [Luke 2:49]

Later, his brothers press him to go to the Feast, reasoning that a public figure cannot rally a following without having high profile visibility at important cultural gatherings. Jesus' response was interesting. He didn't say: "Wow, you're right! How am I going to establish a movement if I don't show the world who I am and what I have to say?" Nor did he say: "Quit giving me your stupid advice! For the last time, I'm not interested in becoming a political leader. Sheesh, you just don't get it!"

As a self-defined person, he says: "The right time for me has not yet come; for you any time is right. The world cannot hate you, but it hates me because I testify that what it does is evil. You go to the Feast. I am not yet going up to this Feast, because for me the right time has not yet come." [John 7:2-8]

My teammates on Novo's reFocusing Team prefer this small modification to Friedman's definition: *"a God-defined person with a non-anxious presence."*

They've developed the *Awaken Workshop* to help Christians study and pray over their lives, relationships, experiences, heart passions, and values for one purpose: to extract from the remarkable investment of God in each life the unique calling that God intends for that person. *Awaken* is nine vigorous, intentional hours dedicated to reveal the clues to who you are and why you're here; the difference you get to make.

How much concentrated time have you devoted to discovering the special impact God intends that you make with your life? [Ephesians 2:10] Is it any wonder you're fuzzy about what God's calling to you might be?

Armed with clarity about her calling, a mature, self-defined leader has little difficulty saying "no." The clearer she becomes, the more willing she is to say "no" to the many good, honorable, helpful opportunities that would take her away from living her central calling from God. She is not upset or threatened when people don't see things the way she does. She does not need the agreement of others to bolster her confidence. She is clear. Decisive. She understands her calling. She is proactive about setting her life up to fulfill *that* calling from God. Unapologetically.

Like Jesus did.

When his buddies encouraged Jesus to take a break, have a good meal, and relax a bit, after his encounter with the Samaritan at the well, he said: *"My food is to do the will of him who sent me and to finish his work."* [John 4:34]

Jesus was clear. Focused. Unfazed.

Self-defined does not mean "workaholic." The mature leader takes full responsibility for her well-being and destiny. Like Jesus, she trusts the Father's goodness, love, and sovereign plan. *She does not look to other people or her circumstances to define her.* Responsible for her own being and destiny, she lives responsibly—even amid a culture that promotes irresponsibility.

Consider Jesus' practice of withdrawing from the press of people and the demands of ministry to commune with the Father, get perspective, and to sleep. Responsible for his own being and destiny, Jesus chose to get away *from those who desperately needed him*: those he could have healed, delivered, taught, and built a bigger, stronger, more powerful ministry around. Why?

Maybe Jesus understood that more than skill, technique, or knowledge, courageous leadership is, most of all, about the *presence of the leader* as he moves through life. To presence himself well with people, Jesus recognized that a vital relationship with the Father, clarity, perspective, and attending to his very appropriate, very human need for rest and refreshing were necessary. Self-definition, like Jesus modeled for us, was the result of his commitment to maturity.

How's yours?

LEADING WITH A NON-ANXIOUS PRESENCE

So far we've said a leader is a self-defined person with a non-anxious presence. In the last section, we unpacked some of what it means to be self-defined, or as my ministry teammates prefer: "*God*-defined." Now, we'll explore what it means to have a non-anxious presence.

Several years ago I was in Kalamazoo, Michigan. We were making final preparations for a four-day character development training that was to commence the next morning. As Ennio Salucci, the lead trainer, and I prepared the volunteer team, he received a phone call. Acknowledging its importance, Ennio stepped away from our preparations for several minutes.

Late that night, after we'd finished with the team, he shared with me the content of that phone call. He'd been struggling with medical symptoms for some time and had a series of tests. Ennio's doctor called to inform him that his tests confirmed the medical team's worst fears: he had chronic lymphocytic leukemia.

Rather than cancelling the training, calling another facilitator to stand in for him, or to log hours on the phone with his wife and doctors, what I witnessed floored me. Ennio prepared me for the next day's training, then gave himself fully and passionately to our participants for the entire four days. Other than our brief conversation, there was no evidence that my friend had received the devastating news. He was clear about why he was alive: to champion those around him to live their lives fully, passionately, and powerfully. Ennio led by example those first days after his diagnosis and for the nearly twenty years that have followed. In that time, Ennio has been in and out of the MD Anderson Cancer Center in Houston more often than I've been to my dentist. And, he's poured his heart and soul into thousands of people in the hundreds of trainings he's conducted since.

To possess a non-anxious presence does not mean to be carefree, laid-back, detached, or disengaged. It means to live with an absence of anxiety. As a powerful squall threatens to swamp their boat, the disciples are a mess. Anxious, fearful, and panicked.

And, Jesus … is … asleep. [Mark 4:38]

Jesus modeled a non-anxious presence perfectly. After benefiting from the miracle of the loaves and fish the crowd wants Jesus to seize political control, overthrow the Romans, and declare himself their King. His response was simply to walk away. Scripture says he withdrew to a solitary place, alone. [Mark 6:46]

A non-anxious presence is easy to carry off when your leadership is well-received, when people are saying great things about you, or when folks are happy and grateful for you, but a non-anxious presence is essential when distress appears omnipresent.

Recall the phrase: "Poor planning on your part does not constitute a crisis on my part."

The less mature are always attempting to enroll others in their disquiet, their "crisis du jour." A perceived catastrophe on the part of certain members of the congregation does not constitute a calamity for a well-defined leader. Do you think for one minute that God, up in Heaven, is wringing His hands over that leaky roof, the lawsuit brought against the church, or the lousy turnout at the society meeting?

I often remind my coaching clients that God is not looking down at them stunned, saying: "Oh my goodness, I didn't see *that* coming!" And, since God is fully aware of your predicament, what do you suppose God wants to do *in you* as a result?

The self-defined leader chooses to interpret these "crises" as precious opportunities to develop mature disciples of Jesus Christ. Friedman is clear: the leader's capacity to contain her own reactivity to the trepidation of others, to avoid becoming polarized, and to self-regulate while staying connected to those who *behave as if in distress* is key to both the leader's differentiation *and* to catalyzing maturity in the culture around her.

Think this through, Christian leader:

- How are you growing in governing your own emotional reactivity? Ask your spouse, your kids, your staff and elders: what evidence do they see of your growth in controlling your reactions when those around you are out of control?

- When individuals or groups are locked in opposition, are you becoming more able to get "altitude," above the fray, and remain curious? Are you getting better at *living in the tension*, without knee-jerking yourself to one side or the other, primarily to exit the pressure of the issue being, as yet, unresolved?

When you react with frustration and anger to the low-tolerance tantrums and angry outbursts of the immature in your ministry context, you've put yourself in *exactly* the same soup! The key is to manage yourself when in conflict and to stay in relationship with those who prefer to attack, blame, and remain irresponsible for their own being and destiny.

It takes stamina to continually define oneself to those who lack self-regulation. Sadly, that kind of stamina is not developed within a culture of cowardice. Nor is it promoted in an American education system that presses for togetherness over against the self- differentiation that is natural when honest competition and healthy individuation is endorsed.

As Friedman noted more than twenty years ago, *most of you are leading chronically anxious emotional dwarfs.* In many systems, the Church has become a hideout for the immature. To me, this is really sad. Of course, there are many reasons why some are emotionally immature. Some of those reasons involve factors beyond their control. People need help with those issues. At the same time, the church doesn't have to coddle people in their immaturity. Instead, those of us in church leadership can call our congregations to something more by reminding them of their identities in Christ. And when believers stand on the promises of Jesus, we can be the most powerful, clear, selfless, and confident people on the planet.

God-defined people with a non-anxious presence.

FOR PERSONAL REFLECTION:

The author observes that the less mature are always attempting to enroll others in their disquiet, whatever their crisis of the moment happens to be. A perceived catastrophe on the part of certain members of the congregation does not constitute a calamity for a well-defined leader.

- Assess your success resisting the anxieties that seem to dominate the immature in your context.

- When was the last time you got sucked into another's disquiet?

- How were you able to regain your peace and confidence? What was your method?

- Recall a time when you managed to maintain altitude when presented with an opportunity to dive into another's anxieties however appropriate they may have been.

- What enabled you to stand non-anxious in that situation?

- Pastors, particularly of small churches, are often conscripted into the commitments of church members, even when the activity has nothing to do with the pastor's calling from God. Reflect on your degree of success declining others' expectations of you.

FOR GROUP DISCUSSION:

Edwin Friedman noted that most leaders in the US are leading "chronically anxious emotional dwarfs." The author of *Leadership Courage* asserts that in many swaths of Christianity the Church has become a hideout for the immature.

- Discuss how applicable you believe each of these statements are to your congregation, ministry, or organization.

- What changes have you noticed in the level of anxiety and immaturity among the "rank and file" in your organization over the last ten and twenty years?

- What is the trend?

- Friedman suggests the *best* way to promote maturity in any system is for the leaders to be self-defined people with a non-anxious presence in the midst of those they lead, regardless of the maturity followers display. Give yourself a letter grade (A-F) for your being God-defined and non-anxious as you carry out your responsibilities in your ministry or work context.

- As you discuss your responses with each other request feedback from others in your group or team about the level of self-definition and non-anxiety they experience from you.

- How could you strengthen one another in becoming more clearly God-defined and non-anxious?

Chapter 6

Responsibility

What does it take to be a courageous leader, particularly amidst a culture that, for decades, has been steeped in cowardice? Can a pastor, denominational executive, or church leader *actually* turn the tide of emotional and spiritual regression before the Church loses what's left of its traction in American society?

We're examining courageous leadership, convinced that God has you reading this book so that you begin to practice a way of being in your life, your business, your marriage, your family, your congregation, and your community for such a time as this.

To review, courageous leadership is not a matter of skill, technique, or knowledge. Its most distinguishing characteristic is the *presence* of the leader as he or she moves through life. So far we've explored what it means to be a self-defined person with a non-anxious presence. Now, we'll turn to a second insight from Friedman—and another attribute that Jesus modeled for us.

Two: Take full responsibility for *your own* emotional being and destiny.

Most pastors struggle here: living as if they were responsible for the emotional being and destiny of dozens, hundreds, or even thousands of other people—and then participating in life as if their own well-being and destiny were dependent on others: the Bishop, their elder board, the denomination, local economic trends, and that abusive control-freak in a position of congregational leadership.

How might pastors and congregations accelerate their progress toward maturity? How might pastors make this single, profound shift?

Let's break it down.

Step one is to disconnect from the generations-long ministerial malpractice of taking responsibility for others. I want to suggest that you and your members can't *both* be responsible for their well-being and destiny. You can, or they can. But both of you cannot. If you take responsibility for them, they won't stand responsible for themselves.

If you don't take responsibility for them, *and instead* you stand with them as if they were responsible before God for their own being and destiny then maybe—just maybe—they will.

How many parents of adult children have lamented their 20-somethings dependence and irresponsibility—until the parents cut off the financial flow?

Faced with the very real possibility of starvation and homelessness, most of those chronically-immature sons and daughters *find a way* to get out of bed, land a job, and struggle their way into responsible adult lives, but the over-responsible parents had to cut down the safety net *first*. To do so, they had to increase their capacity to tolerate the squawks and tantrums of their overly-dependent adult children.

In Matthew 23:37, Jesus mourns for the inhabitants of Jerusalem. When offered comfort, protection, and rescue by the Lord their answer was "no." Jesus is clear: their choice didn't diminish him or the value of the redemption he offered. He was also clear that they would have to live with the consequences of their decision.

So too, pastor, with you.

You are not your church. They are not an extension of you. If you are emotionally healthy, you don't think of yourself as an extension of your spouse, your boss, your siblings, or your district superintendent, do you? Why allow yourself to be enmeshed with your congregation as if *who you are* is determined by their choices and deportment?

Friedman asserts that leaders can bypass burnout by avoiding the trap of taking responsibility for others and their problems. Imagine life without the double bind of being burdened by a false responsibility for the choices and decisions of others. *Scape goat*

Do yourself a favor: re-read Ephesians, I & II Timothy, and Revelation 2:1-7.

Then, answer this:

- Did Paul make himself responsible for Timothy's being and destiny? *No*
- Was Timothy responsible for the being and destiny of the church at Ephesus? *No*

If not, who was?

What *does* Scripture teach?

<u>Step two</u> is to **take full responsibility for *your own* emotional being and destiny**.

Notice how Jesus presences himself when instructing the disciples about his betrayal [Mark 14:18-25]. You don't see him coming apart at the seams, an emotional wreck, begging Judas to reconsider. Instead, he uses the impending calamity *to instruct them* about fidelity, sacrifice, and the cost of discipleship.

At his arrest, Jesus is fully in control of his emotions and reactions. He *does not personalize* Judas' betrayal: "Oh Judas, how could you?" He doesn't negotiate: "Hey fellas, what if I agree to stop teaching in the Temple—would that be OK with you?" Nor does he play the victim: "Doggone it, you guys. If you'd just stayed awake and prayed *like I asked you*, none of this would've happened!" [Mark 14:43-50]

Brought before the Sanhedrin [Mark 14:53-64], Jesus does not throw a tantrum, collapse in an ocean of tears, call down fire, or even expose his accusers' hypocrisy. The only response recorded by Mark is Jesus' unmistakably clear admission that yes, he *is* the Christ, and that they will one day see him sitting at the Father's right hand. This is not to say that Jesus was emotionally repressed. He was a man of sorrows and acquainted with grief. [Isaiah 53:3] He sweat blood the night before his crucifixion. [Luke 22:44] What is critical to note is that Jesus did not make his emotions anyone else's responsibility.

Jesus lived as if his being and destiny were securely and completely in his Father's capable hands. Clear about his calling to serve humankind as he fulfilled the Father's will [Mark 10:45], Jesus' being and destiny was undeterred by the autonomous choices made by the autonomous human beings all around him: Pilate, Peter, Judas, the false accusers before the Sanhedrin, and on and on.

Engaging his life in this way, Jesus catalyzed the maturing of the followers to whom he turned over the Church after his crucifixion. And today, he's turned that Church over to you and me.

FOR PERSONAL REFLECTION:

The author points out that many pastors live as if their well-being and destiny were dependent on others: your Bishop, elder board, denomination, congregation, local economic trends, or an abusively controlling person who is in a position of congregational leadership.

- The author's aspiration is that you take full responsibility for your own emotional being and destiny. How well would you say you are doing this?

- What are the factors that most often undermine your emotional well-being?

- What are the kinds of circumstances that seem to challenge your embrace of your "destiny," as you envision your future?

- If you were able to live as if your being and destiny were securely and completely in your Father's capable hands... how might your health improve?

- How might your marriage and family relationships improve?

- How might the leaders closest to you benefit?

FOR GROUP DISCUSSION:

Edwin Friedman asserts that leaders can bypass burnout by avoiding the trap of taking responsibility for others and their problems. Imagine life without the double bind of being burdened by a false responsibility for the choices and decisions others make.

- How effectively do you as a leadership team, small group, department, or organization eschew the "ministerial malpractice" of taking responsibility for another adult's responsibility?

- When those you lead experience failure how likely are you to shoulder the burden to remove the consequences of their poor decision?

- What are loving alternatives you could begin to practice instead?

The author points out that Jesus, clear about his calling to serve humankind as he fulfilled his Father's will, behaved as if his being and destiny were unaffected by the autonomous choices of those around him.

- How well do you maintain your focus on God's directives to you, regardless of the choices and decisions of those you lead?

- If you were to become a community of leaders who successfully stood responsible for your own being and destiny, how might your organization improve? Collaborate to identify ten beneficial impacts on your church, business, or non-profit.

Challenged by Spiritual Mal practice

This chapter is a Critique on how God's people have integrated (or taught) their identity in Christ, their Mission and purpose with clarity!

A introspective Examination (how much we depend on God), as our Salvation

CHAPTER 7

Differentiation

Now we move from you, the leader, to your organization, church, system, or family.

<u>Three</u>: Promote healthy differentiation within the church or system you lead.

Differentiation means "differentness." Your uniqueness. Your sovereignty as an independent human being. A well-differentiated person takes full responsibility for her own being and destiny. This third principle is an invitation to stand in relationship with your congregants as if they were responsible for their own well-being, which, before God, of course, they are.

Remember how Jesus responded when his disciples were giving themselves to panic? Did he make himself responsible for their emotions, for their sense of well-being, or for their comfort or discomfort? Remember the storm at sea.

In Matthew 14:25-31, the disciples are terrified both by the storm and what they thought to be a "ghost" walking on the water. Still out of the boat, Jesus says: "Take courage! It is I. Don't be afraid." Then, as Peter goes down into the water, Jesus grabs him and asks: "You of little faith, why did you doubt?"

I imagine most pastors, instead, would exclaim something like: "Hey, great job Pete! I am SO VERY PROUD OF YOU! Look *how many* steps you took!! Hey fellas, let's hear it for Peter!"

Jesus' response indicates that he saw this incident as a character-development training opportunity. He interpreted it as a way to prepare Peter and the others for challenges that they would eventually get to confront.

A few years ago, I was caught in a frightening legal matter where jail time and bankruptcy were the most likely outcomes. It took years and hundreds of thousands of dollars to resolve. At one point, with the pressure at its zenith, I was having dinner with my adult kids. When asked how I'd weathered so confounding and threatening a challenge I remember telling them that God had spent the previous sixty-one years preparing me for *this* test.

I've faced many hardships and had experienced God's fidelity in them. Through those difficulties, God had laid the foundation for what was happening in the present. God was still at work developing in me the stamina of faith. I'm so thankful that no one had been able to minimize the challenges that had driven me to my knees at the foot of Jesus' cross!

When members of your church come up against frightening challenges, what is it you think you're doing with and for them? Providing comfort? Encouragement? Appeasement?

Or, are you developing them into mature, godly, Christ-like disciples?

When the disciples are unable to free the boy with the symptoms of epilepsy, Jesus behaves as if they are responsible for their own preparation for ministry: "*This kind can come out only by prayer.*" [Mark 9:29] Jesus seems to believe that "regular Christians" can actually free those who were suffering like this boy was.

My dear friend and mentor, Dr. J. Robert Clinton [retired professor of leadership at the School of Intercultural Studies, Fuller Theological Seminary] taught me what he calls *Goodwin's Expectation Principle*. Essentially, it is this: "People will live up to the expectations of those whom they respect." Jesus seems to have understood this.

Rather than making allowances for their playing small, their love of comfort, and their penchant for control, Jesus behaved as if he expected his followers to live and minister just like he did. He expected them to trust God and step up to the challenges that life presented. Didn't he?

How often and how consistently do you?

For Personal Reflection:

Jesus' response to the storm at sea in Matthew 14 indicates that he saw the incident as a "teachable moment" to strengthen the character of his shipmates. He interpreted it as a way to prepare them for challenges that they would eventually confront.

- When members of your church come up against frightening challenges, what is it you do with and for them? Consider carefully the ways you commonly respond to their predicaments.

- Like Jesus, does it commonly occur to you to challenge them to "take courage?"

- How likely are you to *rebuke* their lack of trust [Matthew 14:31]?

- Fundamentally, do you see yourself as a person tasked with reducing your peoples' anxieties and discouragements OR someone tasked with developing mature Christians who behave like Jesus did?

- What would it require to re-posture yourself more as a people-developer than a caretaker?

For Group Discussion:

It is assumed that these group discussion questions are being processed by leaders of organizations: a denomination, church staff, or executive team who have influence within a business or ministry.

- Discuss how well you have promoted healthy differentiation within the church or system you lead.

- How "risky" have been your attempts to provoke maturity, via differentiation, in your people?

- If you have taken risks in this area, you undoubtedly will have received criticism, frequently, for it. Have you?

- Work together to identify five strategies you might attempt to challenge your people to stand responsible for their own emotional being and destiny.

- If you were to test these strategies with a "pilot group" of emotionally mature members of your organization, with whom would you choose to work?

CHAPTER 8

Stand

If the Church in North America is to become fully alive, awake, and influential, her pastors must become what they were always intended by God to be.

Courageous leaders.

So far, we've offered:

<u>One</u>: Courageous leadership is not about skill, technique, or knowledge. It is, most of all, about the *presence* of the leader as he or she moves through life.

<u>Two</u>: Take full responsibility for your own emotional being and destiny.

<u>Three</u>: Promote healthy differentiation within the church or system you lead.

To this we add a fourth leadership characteristic:

Stand, as an exemplar, in the sabotage and backlash that must come.

We've been looking at the way Jesus embodied these traits—not for intellectual edification, but to challenge you, Christian leader, to change.

As a minister of the Gospel of Christ *you are an exemplar*. Your way of life *is* a model. It must be so. It is ridiculous to serve in Christian ministry and to shrink from the exposure and vulnerability befitting your station. A leader stands. Sometimes that means you get to stand, alone. Always it means you are visible in ways that those who follow are not. My invitation is to embrace the reality and necessity of standing up, of standing out, and of standing alone or *get out* of Christian ministry.

There is an anxiety, common to American culture, about standing alone. It seems that only raving narcissists are immune from this. I disagree. There is another kind of person who has calmed her own disquiet when coming under scrutiny—or fire. It is the kind of leader we're examining in this book.

Consider the accounts that appear in John 6: five thousand people witness the miracle of the loaves and fish, Jesus walks on the Sea of Galilee, and a sizeable crowd follows him to the other side. He calls them out! "You're only here for the show; because of the miracles." This is how he *greets* them!

Then he exposes their shallowness with his seldom-repeated "sermon in the synagogue" where he speaks about eating his body and drinking his blood. [John 6:53] The crowd scatters, and many of his disciples turned back and no longer followed him.

Does Jesus backtrack, and explain that his words were just hyperbole, a figure of speech? Does he beg them to return? Does he capitulate, soften the message, lower the bar, or take *any* steps to ease their distress? Read the end of John 6 and see for yourself!

A few chapters later, Jesus has become *so popular* that even the Greeks are seeking him out. [John 12:20-24] They ask Philip for an audience with the Master.

At this moment, Jesus, and those close to him, appear to be at the pinnacle of popularity. Imagine Philip's enthusiasm as he tells Andrew the great news. The two go together to let Jesus know that "so-and-so" has requested an audience with Rabbi Jesus. Rather than seizing upon his mushrooming popularity and assigning one of them to begin scheduling his appointments with dignitaries, notice what Jesus does. *He completely ignores the request.* Instead, he talks to the two of them about his impending sacrificial death.

"Unless a grain of wheat falls to the ground and dies…" [John 12:24]

Neither the admiration nor the disdain of the crowds and his closest followers deters Jesus from his mission. Jesus does not simply *take* a stand. He *is* a stand. Having taken full responsibility, before the Father, for his being and destiny, Jesus lives as if his every movement, his attitudes, his words, and even his silence are on purpose. His is the Father's purpose to establish the Kingdom of God in the lives of women and men. This is what leaders do.

Acclimate yourself to the rigor of taking total responsibility, before God, for your own responses to your environment and circumstances. Friedman notes: "Leaders must not only not be afraid of that position, but they must come to love it."

You ask: Where do I get that kind of courage? How could I ever come to *love* being ridiculed and adored, being evaluated and critiqued and judged all the time?

What if you have it all, already?

What if you've been given the capacity to stand in this rigor, as an exemplar to those you lead? What if you have it *in Christ*? If anyone is in Christ, he is a new creation, remember? [I Corinthians 5:17] God's power has given us *everything we need* for life and godliness, remember? [2 Peter 1:3]

A leader is not simply someone who gets things done or who gets other people to behave in desirable ways. A leader *is* different. She presences herself in life and relationships in a uniquely beneficial way. This uniqueness transcends behavior, skill, and knowledge. It can best be described in terms of *being*.

A courageous leader's way-of-being is distinctive. *It provokes maturity* in those she influences. The differences are palpable.

One difference is the way a leader *is* in the midst of sabotage and backlash. My mentor Dr. J. Robert Clinton has identified *Leadership Backlash* to be one of the most common methods God uses to develop leadership character. Backlash occurs when once-enthusiastic followers turn against their leader in the face of unexpected difficulties.

In *A Failure of Nerve*, Edwin Friedman elaborates: "Mutiny and sabotage came... from colleagues whose will was sapped by unexpected hardships along the way." It is the leader's person and posture amidst this collegial sabotage that is so stunningly effective.

A courageous leader recognizes how common backlash and sabotage is, and both are the product of evacuated courage in those disheartened by difficulty. The leader interprets backlash as an opportunity to model a way of leading that inspires confidence [from the Latin, literally "*with trust*"] toward God, and deepens the maturity and faithfulness of colleagues and followers. Further, this kind of leader chooses to interpret the opposition as *provision from Heaven.*

Consider Jesus.

In John 6:66 we read that *many* of Jesus' disciples turned back and no longer followed him. Immediately, Jesus turns to the twelve and asks: Don't you want to go away too? He saw the departure of the many as an opportunity to test the resolve of the leaders closest to him.

Embracing the reality of God's sovereignty and apprehending the security of God's unconditional love, a leader *leans into the resistance* with a posture of confident curiosity. "God has this!" she might remind herself while stepping toward those who, unnerved by fear, have just betrayed her. This may shock you: it is the leader's *humility* that creates the opening to presence himself so resourcefully.

Just a few verses later, Jesus is teaching in the temple courts. When those who hear him begin to applaud his brilliance, he says: "My teaching is not my own. It comes from him who sent me. If anyone chooses to do God's will, he will find out whether my teaching comes from God or whether I speak on my own. He who speaks on his own does so to gain honor for himself, but he who works for the honor of the one who sent him is a man of truth." [John 7:17] This is humility.

The leader recognizes that he is not powerful enough to have caused the upset nor the circumstances that many say disturb them. Aware that each person connected to the disappointment has a contribution, he faces little temptation to assume he alone is responsible for the unwelcome turn of events. He has grounded himself in the understanding that *he is not significant enough* to have produced the organization's successes *or* its failures. He has a part. His colleagues have a part. The system has a part, and factors beyond anyone's control have also contributed to the outcome.

Rather than encouraging carelessness, the leader's decision to interpret life this way empowers responsibility to one another and to the ministry's mission and goals.

Scapegoating, so common in an anxious, immature culture, is antithetical to the stand of the leader and the developing ethos of the organization. Even when the less mature succumb to its pull, the leader is not provoked to respond in kind.

Keeping in mind how consequential it is to shift the culture of any church, the leader has developed stamina to live into Paul's charge in 1 Corinthians 16:13-14: *"Be on your guard; stand firm in the faith; be men of courage; be strong..."*

I love the ancient King James rendering of this verse: *"Quit ye like men."*

FOR PERSONAL REFLECTION:

The author asserts that a leader sometimes stands alone. You always are visible in ways that those who follow are not. The invitation is to embrace the reality and necessity of standing up, standing out, and standing alone—or *get out* of Christian ministry.

- To what degree is this a struggle for you? Give yourself a letter grade (A-F) on your willingness to stand in life as an example for others to emulate.
- Which is more difficult for you: standing up, standing out, or standing alone?
- When have you taken a stand that required courage and were vindicated by God?
- What, in your character, was strengthened through the experience?
- How often do you use yourself as an example of what it means to stand for Christ?

FOR GROUP DISCUSSION:

In John Chapter 12 Jesus' popularity appears to be peaking. Important gentiles are seeking him out. Rather than seizing the opportunity to swell the ranks of followers, Jesus points his disciples to his impending death as he teaches them: "Very truly I tell you, unless a kernel of wheat falls to the ground and dies, it remains only a single seed. But if it dies, it produces many seeds." [John 12:24]

- To what degree has your organization embraced the "more is better" philosophy that seems to be ever-present in the North American Church?
- What is a more biblically-consistent alternative?

- How readily do you embrace both growth *and* decline as opportunities to teach your people (and yourselves) about God's priorities?

The author challenges leaders to acclimate to the rigor of taking total responsibility, before God, for your own responses to your circumstances. He then quotes Friedman: "Leaders must not only not be afraid of that position, but they must come to love it."

- To what degree have you come to *love* being fully responsible for your response to your surroundings and circumstances?
- What could you do, as colleagues, to encourage one another to love living in this rigor?

CHAPTER 9

Motivation

What kind of minister will lead the Church in our day to salt and light the world?

Pastor, what can you do to arouse your church from its slumber and stand in the storm of insolence and juvenility that such a stirring will provoke?

We've been examining what it means to live and lead courageously amidst a culture of cowardice that, from my perspective, has captured the Church in North America, leaving American society rudderless in a tsunami of sensuality, secularism, and self-centeredness.

Edwin Friedman informs our fifth concept: **Don't "push on the rope:" the unmotivated are invulnerable to insight**.

I've done a little boating. One summer in Leland, Michigan, you might have seen me standing on a dock, tugging on a line, endeavoring to center the hull of our friends' Boston Whaler over the submerged bunks of a small boatlift. Without thinking, I push my hand out, as if the boat will somehow move away from me.

It's as if I've imagined that the rope has somehow stiffened so that it can propel the boat away from the dock and over the lift. Of course, it doesn't. It can't. You cannot provoke change by *pushing on a rope.*

Friedman offers this: the unmotivated are invulnerable to insight.

Yet, weekend after weekend, well-intentioned ministers stand in pulpits all over the land, bringing scintillating insights from God's Word, hoping that *learning will motivate life change.*

Statistics, sadly, illuminate the truth of the matter. People, by and large, are *not* changed—at least, not much.

Too many of those who listen are invulnerable to insight. *Without compelling motivation, there is insufficient hunger to embrace the price and pain of change.* Even change that sounds good, change that would be preferable to the status quo, or change that could propel the listener toward an honorable outcome will elicit mental agreement. And, it will not ignite action.

What's the key?

Think about Jesus' parable of the farmer. [Mark 4:3-20] The key to fruitfulness is *the soil…*not the seed. Yet, we in pastoral ministry devote hundreds of our most valuable hours fussing over the seed—while ignoring the soil.

Does that make sense to you?

Look at it again: "Some people are like seed along the path, where the word is sown. As soon as they hear it, Satan comes and takes away the word that was sown in them. Others, like seed sown on rocky places, hear the word and at once receive it with joy. But since they have no root, they last only a short time. When trouble or persecution comes because of the word, they quickly fall away. Still others, like seed sown among thorns, hear the word; but the worries of this life, the deceitfulness of wealth and the desires for other things come in and choke the word, making it unfruitful. Others, like seed sown on good soil, hear the word, accept it, and produce a crop—some thirty, some sixty, some a hundred times what was sown." [Mark 4:15-20]

Jesus' directs our attention to *the condition of the soil.* "Some people are…" he begins. The unmotivated are invulnerable to insight.

So, why is it that we devote ourselves to sifting, sorting, cleaning, massaging, and polishing the seed? Sermon preparation in post-Enlightenment Christendom consumes the largest portion of most Evangelical pastors' workweeks. When I was in seminary, my preaching professor told me to invest an hour in preparation for every minute in the pulpit. Thirty hours preparation for a thirty-minute message. Imagine that! Thirty of my fifty-five-hour workweek spent *away from my people,* away from preparing the soil of their hearts, and away from provoking their hunger for God's Word.

I began to ask myself why pastors give so little attention to tilling the soil of their hearer's hearts?

Could it be that we've forgotten what business we're in?

Maybe we've inadvertently supplanted the make-mature-disciples-who-live-like-Jesus business with the faithfully-proclaim-the-Word-of-God-business. Yes, you and I have been commissioned to faithfully proclaim God's Word, but we do it *so that* people around us live like Jesus.

Don't we?

To distill the ministry of the Gospel down to faithful proclamation without *equal regard* to the life-changing results of our preaching is akin to straining gnats and swallowing camels. If the unmotivated are invulnerable to insight and if the key to fruitfulness is the condition of the soil, wouldn't it be wise to get *really, really good* at soil preparation?

Several years ago I was in Honolulu in training with a catalytic Christian character development ministry. I'd been an "apprentice" for what seemed like an eternity. It was late at night, and Dan Tocchini, my mentor, walked with me as we trudged slowly through the parking garage.

I was feeling defeated... confused... perplexed. He'd given me the opportunity to facilitate a number of crucial conversations with seminar participants, and the conversations had not gone well. At one point, Dan had caught my eye as I was engaged in *what I thought* was a supportive and helpful conversation with one of our participants. He motioned me back to the table where he sat. As I approached, I realized he was tapping his finger on a post-it note he'd stuck to the table. When I got close enough, I saw the words: "SHUT UP! YOU DON'T KNOW WHAT YOU'RE DOING"

I clearly had missed it, and I didn't know why. Crestfallen and unsure, I flopped in the chair he'd vacated.

Late that night as we walked silently to our car, my head was still spinning. What Dan said to me next changed my life. I recount it in the hope that it will change yours as well.

He said: "Kirk, you keep handing people fish." "We are not here to give people fish. And we are not here to teach people how to fish. *We are here to provoke their hunger.*"

When a person is hungry enough, she will feed herself. If fishing is the way, she will teach herself to fish, or find someone to show her how, or find a way to get fish out of the lake and onto her family's dinner table.

In study after study conducted in Western Europe, welfare recipients did not find jobs until *after* the government's assistance ran out. Then, *almost immediately* they found work.

Hungry enough, they were no longer unmotivated. Motivated, they were *vulnerable* to insight.

They discovered. They learned. They changed. They took risks. They found work, and they kept working in the jobs they got. They fed themselves and their families. Starvation did not skyrocket. Neither, according to what I've read, did crime.

The motivated *are* vulnerable to insight.

What might occur if you got really good at provoking your parishioners' hunger for God's Word?

What if, this coming year, you devoted yourself to provoking their hunger for maturity?

What if you saw to it that your parish became a more *uncomfortable* place to stay spiritually and emotionally immature?

You might get to reinvent yourself in the process. You would have the opportunity to trust Jesus in ways you haven't in a long time. You could trade familiar patterns and skills for fresh, provocative, people-changing ones.

Remember the thirst you *once* had to learn to preach, lead a staff, or work well with elders and trustees? When you had no idea what to do, you were motivated to stretch, to risk, to try as-yet unproven approaches, and when they failed, you learned from them. You stayed close enough to people that they "got" your heart. Because you did they trusted you as you and they experimented together.

But now, a decade or two later, you've found ways to avoid the riskiness of early ministry. You've erected well-identified "guardrails" on your ministry. Staying safely within the rails, much of ministry flows according to plan. Of course, there are always those outliers, when people you assumed were mature and dependable prove to be anything but. Yet, aside from the occasional meltdown by a volunteer, ministry is predictable. And achingly uninspiring!

Imagine becoming a spiritual provocateur—like Jesus was—in your ministry context. What if you challenged your people the way he challenged his?

Why wouldn't you?

Tick, tock...

PIONEERS, BELONGERS, AND RESISTERS

In more than thirty years of ministry—most of it to ministers— it is stunning how much of a pastor's time, thoughts, and prayers are consumed with *those who are the least motivated to follow.*

While you are breaking yourself to provide compelling insight to inspire the unmotivated, they are breaking your will to lead. They are standing in the way of the change you believe God wants. They are preventing the advance of God's Kingdom in your city.

Once the pastor's will has been broken, it's "lights out" for that church. When that happens, it's also "lights out" for those outside. God assembled your congregation to be His redemptive provision for the community around you. When your church surrenders to the selfish demands of the least mature among you, the neighborhood and city you were meant to illuminate with the lived-and-proclaimed Gospel remains darkened.

Pastor, your courageous, decisive leadership is that important. Your will, your resolve, and your stamina in the face of opposition from people you love dearly, is essential to the Kingdom's advance in American society.

This concept is offered so you'll avoid the energy sapping, confidence-draining effect of the unmotivated on your leadership *if* you are motivated enough to change.

To lead, you can't "push on the rope."

Rather than focusing on those most resistant to your leadership, give yourself to the people who are most willing to go with you. Give *them* your time, your creativity, and your energy.

Working with scores of churches across the country in dozens of denominations, I've had the opportunity to watch thousands of Christians respond to change. As I have, I've made a rather startling observation, that I've been testing for more than a decade. See what you think.

My thesis is this: *People have trained themselves, over their lifetime, as to how they respond to change.* Your job is to accurately assess where each of your key people are and lead them through change based on their individual change posture. In any community, I suggest you'll find that people will posture themselves in one of three ways.

There are some in your congregation who have trained themselves to take risks, to try new, untested possibilities, to leap into the unknown *just to see if something better can result.* Their focus is almost exclusively on the merits of the change you propose. Once they are convinced that the change is preferable to the status quo they will embrace the change you propose.

These people are **"pioneers."** They are God's gift to you!

The majority in any established congregation, however, are not pioneers. They are what I call **"belongers."**

The belongers are God's gift to you as well! They build community. They are stabilizers. Many of these folks are wonderfully reliable workers in the bowels of your organization. But, over their lifetimes, they've trained themselves to move *with the group*, and not in front of it or behind it. It's important for a belonger to fit in—or, more precisely, *to not stand out*.

Pioneers, by contrast, don't care at all about fitting in. They're not worried about standing out, because *pioneers simply want to make a difference.*

However, belongers are a different breed. Not bad. Not good. Just different. A belonger is willing to change when two conditions are met. *Belongers will embrace change when they're convinced that it is safe and successful to do so*—and not before. And, herein is the rub. Pastors keep wanting their belongers to be on the leading edge of change. The trouble is, they never have, and they never will!

No change *at first* is guaranteed to succeed, nor is it absolutely certain that people won't get hurt in one way or another if they embrace a proposed change.

Pastors all over the land exhaust themselves trying to inspire, encourage, cajole, and manipulate the great many belongers who are faithfully laboring inside their churches in the hope that they will embrace change along with the pioneers.

They don't. They won't. It's not in their nature or their training to put themselves at risk like that.

You will never find a belonger on the leading-edge of change!

This leaves a third group. I call them **"resisters."** These are the people whose primary orientation in life is *pain avoidance.* They've trained themselves to steer clear of the possibility of loss, whenever they can. It's important that your "resisters" avoid being wrong. For them, it is essential not to fail. Thus, resisters are unlikely to implement *any* change that can be avoided or delayed.

They too, are God's gift to you! They are steady. They are loyal. They're likely to show up whenever the doors are open. Traditionalists, they engage in church life in much the same way people have for fifty years or more. They *still* tithe.

Resisters and pioneers interpret life in mutually exclusive ways. When a pioneer is confronted with an opportunity, as soon as she sees the *possibility of improvement*, her default is: "Why not?" The resister will intuit the possibility of failure or loss and think: "Why take an imprudent risk?" The belonger will be hesitant, moving only when the group decides it will be safe.

The culture that's been established in your congregation will determine how predominant each group is. Sadly, churches are one of the few places in American society where resisters often congregate en masse. I suppose government is the other. I'm thinking here about bureaucrats, not politicians.

Contrary to almost everything you've ever read about leadership, I want to assert, that a great leader is not one who somehow inspires belongers to become pioneers, or resisters to transform into belongers.

No.

A great leader is one who leads her or his people appropriately.

Jesus made invitations, then watched how people chose to respond: pioneer, belonger, or resister. Like Jesus, effective leaders will lead their pioneers a certain way, their belongers another way, and their resisters a third way.

Here's what I mean:

Pastor, live with your pioneers! Make sure they populate your appointment calendar. Every week, ensure that you spend *most* of your time with pioneers.

Work to clear your calendar of resisters, and to fill it with pioneers. It may take three months or more to wean yourself away from the passion-extinguishing complaints and tantrums of the unmotivated. Do it. Begin now.

Proactively schedule your office appointments with those who are most responsive to your leadership. Invest generously in their lives. Take risks together. Experiment. Face the challenges that arise together. Support them as they grow in their willingness to trust God and as their character rapidly grows to mirror that of Christ. You'll enjoy your life and ministry a *lot* more, and greater Kingdom fruit will be born, as well.

Nine months from now, you could be *leaping* into your work week with a vigor, optimism, and enthusiasm that most of your folks have *never seen in you.*

LEADING YOUR PEOPLE APPROPRIATELY

Watching hundreds and hundreds of ministers struggle to lead their people has been breathtaking. Breaking from the example of effective leaders in every other human endeavor, pastors focus their efforts on those who are *least motivated* to follow.

No wonder the burnout rate in the pastorate is dwarfed only by the dropout rate.

The most effective ministry leaders I know live with the congregation's pioneers. Pastor, ask your pioneers about their passions for the things

God has laid on your heart. Listen for alignment between your vision and theirs, your heart and theirs, your passions and theirs. *This area of overlap is where you and they get to play!*

Pray with them. Dream with them. If your hope is to touch the unchurched, envision the kinds of impact you'd most want to have on the lives of those you'll serve. Imagine yourselves serving authentically, regularly, and generously for their benefit.

Do some planning and strategizing, but *please* don't get a brain cramp trying to figure it all out in advance. Excessively planning for ministry is an almost irresistible temptation for church people. Don't waste your vigor over-planning in the comfort of your church conference room.

Quick, before you lose your nerve, get out of the church and begin to bless people. Thrust yourself into action with your pioneers. Get off the property. Meet with civic leaders. Learn where your congregation can help, where you can make a God-honoring difference, and go after it. Love people. Serve them.

For Heaven's sake, experiment. Incubate.

Pilot. Test. Adjust.

Go-again, fearlessly *and* flexibly.

When what you try doesn't work—*do something else.*

Do *anything* else.

Let these be rich times of learning and of enjoying the adventure together.

As you and your pioneers love and care for the unchurched *in ways that bless their lives*, those you serve will be skeptical, initially. They'll be wary that church people would serve without a hidden agenda, a "gotcha," a hook.

As you continue to be with them for their benefit, and not for yours, their skepticism will be replaced with gratitude.

When those you serve express their appreciation, communicate this broadly through the congregation. Your belongers will be listening!

Raise the visibility of your pioneers. Make them your congregation's "heroes" and make a big deal of their willingness to risk, innovate, and lead in the change *especially* when a new attempt fails. Celebrate that too.

Over time, your belongers will decide that it *is* beneficial and safe to join in. Have places prepared, ready for them to serve. Plan these in advance. Eventually, more and more belongers will embrace the change, until it becomes the "new normal" for your congregation.

All the while, another amazing transformation is taking place. As you continue serving the unchurched, from a place of humility and unconditional love, their gratitude will be accompanied by openness. *When they ask* about your relationship with God, then you answer.

"Always be prepared to give an answer to everyone who asks you to give the reason for the hope that you have." [1 Peter 3:15]

The key, Pastor, is to disproportionately invest your time and attention in the pioneers, the risk-takers, and the adventurers. Suspend your impulse to convince the resisters and to involve the belongers on the leading edge of change. They will watch from afar, and once it seems safe to them, they will begin to play.

In the meantime, have a blast with your pioneers. Make a difference in the lives of those you're serving. Enjoy what God does.

Hooray!

FOR PERSONAL REFLECTION:

In this chapter, you were invited to remember the thirst *you once had* to learn to minister, or to manage, and to lead others. Recall how you once were motivated to stretch, to risk, and to try new things. When they failed, you learned from them. Early on, you stayed close enough to people to make sure they got your heart. They trusted you while you experimented, together.

- What prices would you likely pay to return to the degree of experimentation and rapid learning you experienced early in your career?
- How would you benefit, personally?
- How would your organization improve?
- What psychological or attitudinal "guardrails" have you erected that keep your work predictable *and* uninspiring?
- Name a dozen people you could open your heart to, sharing hopes and dreams for whatever it is you do together.

FOR GROUP DISCUSSION:

The author asserts that people, by and large, have trained themselves all their lifetimes as to how they respond to change. And, almost all the time, they respond to change opportunities in predictable ways. Pioneers respond one way. Belongers a second way. And, resisters a third. As leaders, your job is not to convert people from one posture to another. Your job is to notice how your people are trained to respond, and to lead them accordingly.

- Discuss how well these the descriptions match your experience of people across your lifetime.

- The primary distinction between belongers and pioneers is that the former will not embrace change until they believe it will be safe and successful to do so. A pioneer cares little about safety or the likelihood of success, basing her engagement on the virtues of the anticipated "new normal" should the change succeed. Discuss whether you see yourself primarily as a pioneer, belonger, or resister. Collaborate until you all can agree as to which category best describes each of your responses to change.

- One of the best indicators is the question you ask when a change opportunity arises. "What will it cost me? Will this hurt? Do *I* have to change?" are naturally occurring responses of resisters. "How do you know it'll work? What are the risks? Who's done it before and how did it go for them?" are questions common to belongers. Pioneers will ask: "tell me more about the benefits that could result. How good might this be? What if we all got onboard? How can I help?" With this clarification, review your conclusions about each other.

- Identify twenty key people in your congregation or organization, and work together to decide whether each is a pioneer, belonger, or resister.

Chapter 10

The Adventurous Life

Where and when did the role of pastor become so closely associated with the characteristics of *terrible leadership*: anemic, people-pleasing, comfort-oriented, weakness-honoring, safety-bound, consensus-collecting, approval-seeking, distress-abating caretaking?

How did we get from the decisive, principle-inspired boldness of Jesus with the money-changers [Matthew 21], Paul and the riot in Ephesus [Acts 19], and Peter on the first Pentecost [Acts 2], to *this*?

Consider the frightening judgment of Ananias and Sapphira [Acts 5], the way the power of God rested on Stephen at his stoning [Acts 6], and the arrest of early church leaders for "turning the world upside down" [Acts 17:6].

How have we settled for a religious experience so predictable, routinized, and boring that men of any age, and people under the age of 40 stay away in droves?

You might remember a *Flo TV* ad that debuted in a Super Bowl a while back. Sports announcer, Jim Nance voice-overs the sad spectacle of Jason Glasby being led around the lingerie department by his girlfriend. Nance says: *"Hello, friends. We have an injury report on Jason Glasby. As you can see, his girlfriend has removed his spine, rendering him incapable of watching the game."*

I'm wondering about the injury report on the Church in North America. *Who has removed our spine?*

To lead your church well pastor, **re-introduce yourself to *the adventurous life.*** Edwin Friedman, in *A Failure of Nerve,* observed: "What our civilization needs most is leaders with a bold sense of adventure… Our nation's obsession with safety ignores the fact that every American alive today benefits from centuries of risk-taking by previous generations… every modern benefit from health to enjoyment to production has come about because Americans in previous generations put adventure before safety."

Do you find incomprehensible the pathway from the behavior of the Church described in the Book of Acts and that of most any Sunday morning gathering in the US today?

How on earth did the Church get from being a vibrant, exciting, world overturning, status-quo challenging, and Kingdom of God-advancing powerhouse to predictable, regimented, backward-looking, tradition-bound, safety-dominant, repository of religious relics?

When were ministers of the Gospel transformed from courageous, God-trusting, whole-hearted, catalytic change agents to providers of religious education and entertainment, chaplains of religious tradition, scholar-rhetoricians, and caregivers to the devout?

Consider Jesus' experience. Born how? Where? When? His incarnation was *an adventure.* [Luke 2:1-38] As a little kid, he ventures off from his family to hang with the teachers in the temple courts. He's on his own for three days—at twelve-years-old. [Luke 2:41-50] His childhood was *an adventure.* Then, at thirty, he is led *by God's Spirit* into the wilderness where Satan challenges, tests, mocks, and opposes him for almost six weeks. [Luke 4:1-13] Remember?

On his return, he's in the temple on Sabbath and the scroll of Isaiah is *handed to him.* He reads a portion, says a very few words and sits back down. The people who heard him "were furious," forcefully removed him from town, and attempted to murder him by casting him over a cliff. [Luke 4:16-29]

You may have forgotten that Jesus "emptied himself" of his divinity to the degree that he had to figure stuff out in the moment. [Philippians 2:6-8] Why do you think he knelt to scratch in the sand when the angry religious mob was about to hurl rocks at the woman who'd had the affair? [John 8:6] Could it be that he had to hear from his Father to know what to do next? [John 5:19] He had to suffer every temptation as a fully-human human being. He *learned obedience* through the things he suffered. [Hebrews 5:8] Jesus showed us the adventurous life.

When facing important decisions, the Son of God *had to* withdraw to pray. This wasn't just an "exercise" to demonstrate for us the prayer life we're to have. He *needed* to receive insight from his Father. [Luke 6:12-13] His life, the life he modeled for us, was an *adventure.*

Was not his experience in the garden of Gethsemane an adventure? I suggest that Jesus had no idea Peter would lop off the soldier's ear! In classic "Jesus form," he used this as a teaching moment about how citizens of his Father's Kingdom were to live. [John 18:10-11]

What has become of *adventure* in your life, pastor?

I'm not advocating that you risk for the thrill of it, that you put yourself in harm's way for the emotional rush some get when they do dangerous things, or that you behave erratically just to break up the boredom. I'm inviting you to the adventurous life *for the advancement of God's reign and rule* in your community. This is not adventure for adventure's sake. It's returning to the biblically normal life of risk and trust as we presence the way of Jesus in a culture more dark and desperate than any of us may fully appreciate.

THE ADVENTUROUS LIFE

What an adventure it could be to...

- Trust Christ as you call people to distinctively demonstrate the way of Jesus to the world.
- Trust the Father as you lead your people off the church campus to love people and meet real needs in your community.
- Trust the Holy Spirit as you confront sin so clearly and confidently that those you influence regain their capacity to blush. [Jeremiah 6:15]
- Love your spouse so consistently and spectacularly that no one would wonder if the congregation had taken her spot in your heart.

- Invite your people to take responsibility for their own well-being and destiny in Christ, serving *their* commitment to mature in Christ-likeness.

- Break up whatever fallow ground remains in your own heart [Jeremiah 4:3], to commit to love as if you've never been hurt [Luke 23:34], to reach to reconcile with those from whom you're now estranged [Romans 12:18]…and do it all in full view of your congregation, so they can learn to live like Jesus *from your example* as well as your preaching [1 Peter 5:3].

What might be gained were you to love that problematic elder enough to challenge the irritating and demeaning way he engages those around him?

What benefits would accrue if you were *really* to champion your people to a lifestyle of financial sacrifice until it becomes the norm? What do you think we in the Church are perpetuating when 60-80% of long-time church attendees give **nothing** in return for the services and benefits they receive? When fewer than ten percent of Church members actually tithe?

Why, I wonder, do pastors take pride in attendance numbers when *most* of those we count contribute neither time nor money to the welfare of the community of faith, let alone the waiting and watching community outside our doors?

If you are in the religious education and entertainment business I can understand why you'd eschew adventure and risk, but if you're in the people-development business, committed to make mature followers of Jesus, there's really no other way.

Is there?

LIVING ADVENTUROUSLY REQUIRES RISK

As it is with *any* adventure, there is always the possibility of failure, loss, injury, embarrassment, being mistaken, and getting hurt.

The Church today seems to have so little tolerance for the latter that it's unwilling to engage the former. And, this reality is absolutely *stunning* in light of the Biblical record. The Christian life is *anything* but safe, cautious, predictable, measured, and reasonable. Everywhere in the Bible, those who followed God were *adventurers*.

By contrast, imagine this scene: more than 5,000 have come out to the wilderness to hear Jesus speak. Eventually it dawns on the disciples that if the crowds don't get something to eat, some will grow faint, maybe ill. When Jesus sees that all they have on hand is five loaves and two fish, he pats the young boy on the head and exclaims: "Oh my gosh! We have to *shut this meeting down right now* so everyone can get home to eat and rest. From now on, we must hold these gatherings where people can get plenty of nourishing food, refreshments and medical services. Let's be sure to schedule plenty of breaks so people don't overextend themselves."

Consider this situation: Jesus is about to send the disciples out two-by-two. He gives them these instructions: "Be sure you take plenty of money with you and arrange your lodgings well in advance. When you enter a new village, if they're happy you're there, stay briefly, so you don't wear out your welcome. And, if there's *any* resistance at all, leave quickly and quietly. For goodness sake, don't stir anything up!"

Picture Peter and John hurrying to the temple past a disabled person who is begging. They avoid eye contact and, as they pass, simply shrug their shoulders. One is overheard telling the other: "So sad that the government doesn't take care of the indigent, isn't it?"

Imagine that the disciples are attempting to cross the Galilee with Jesus asleep below deck. Ever cautious, they hug the shore *just in case* a squall appears. Sure enough, a storm does arise! Alarmed, they awaken Jesus who screams out in terror: "Quick, hand me a lifejacket! We've *got to* get to shore right away! These waves will probably capsize us! We must <u>never</u> travel by boat again. It is *just too dangerous!*"

Read through the Gospels, the Book of Acts, the Epistles and then the entire Old Testament. *You'll see God's people continually in peril.*

Sometimes, God tells them to do what's impossible—like instructing Gideon to reduce his forces *before* going to war against a far more formidable foe. Other times, God's people find themselves in circumstances where they have no hope but for a miracle. The Egyptian army chasing the Israelite slaves to the shores of the Red Sea, for example.

God keeps putting his people in *unreasonable* situations. They keep ending up in circumstances where they *have to* trust God. Where they can't rely on themselves.

They're living *the adventurous life.*

THE ADVENTURE OF BEING IN OVER YOUR HEAD

Why is the Christian life such an adventure? What has your experience been, following diligently after God, as best you know?

In my life, I repeatedly find myself in dilemmas that are completely beyond my ability. This was far less common before I surrendered my life to Christ.

Now, the adventurous life beacons everywhere.

It seems that God wants me in water just over my head where I get to trust him as a way of life. Something inside urges me to sprint into the center of my untidy life and to look for God *there*, as my provision.

As I've journeyed with Jesus these "adventures" have occurred dozens of times. Here are a few of the more memorable examples:

- As a consultant, while traveling to meet the elders and staff of a conflicted church, I discover I've been completely misinformed about the severity of the situation into which I'm about to step. *All* that I've prepared for three days of meetings must be scrapped, and there's no time to develop a new plan. I go anyway, crying out to God from my seat on the plane.

- Early in my business career, I'm in my *first* manager's meeting. Our company president has instructed all the department managers to violate the terms of a licensing agreement. All the managers nod in agreement. Knowing this could cost me my promotion I address my objections to our president.

- While leading a Bible study, I'm summoned to the phone and learn my son has been in jail for two days, out of state, and unable to reach me. I can't speak with him, and what few details I've been given about what's happened are perplexing. I book a flight to leave the next morning.

- Sitting in church listening to a sermon on the eighth commandment, I'm immediately reminded of a situation nearly a decade before where I failed to honor the Lord in an employment agreement. I have the sense that I'm to make restitution in the form of a five-figure sum. I write the check and pen a letter of repentance, explaining my disobedience to my former CEO.

- On vacation with Annie and our sons I learn of the accidental death overseas of someone *very* dear to me. Next of kin have yet to be notified. It becomes clear that the Lord wants me to deliver

the awful news. I swallow my own shock and grief, repack my
suitcase, and grab a cab to the airport.

- I'm riding a ski lift with an unusually amorous couple when two
  thoughts I can't shake enter my head: this man is not with his
  wife, and I'm going to give him a stern warning "from God."
  After wrestling with the Lord, I introduce myself and deliver the
  message.

- Delivering groceries to the needy, I learn that a woman for whom
  we'd prayed has been cured of a severe infection. She insists that
  we immediately go to see her friend. On the way, I learn that her
  friend is dying of brain cancer. We go anyway. I lay my hands on
  the woman's head and pray for her healing.

- Another executive and I have been placed in direct competition
  for a significant promotion only one of us can have. We are polar
  opposites by almost every metric. Months in, the Lord indicates
  I'm to repent to my colleague, bow out of the competition, and
  pledge my willingness to support him as my boss. I walk into his
  office and ask his forgiveness.

- After a training event I'm told that one of my attempts at
  humor was deeply offensive to a group of leaders there. I take
  responsibility for my impact, express remorse for my insensitivity,
  and repent to those I've affronted.

- Driving from church to a Father's Day celebration, traffic is
  inching past police cars and a fire engine positioned to block the
  view of drivers from a particularly gruesome accident. Glancing to
  my right I see the wreckage of a blue Mustang convertible.
  It is the car my daughter and son were driving! The car has flipped
  onto the hood, windshield flattened. There is no room for a
  human to have survived. Driver and passenger must have been
  thrown from the car or decapitated.

There can be no other explanation.

Crying out to God, I jerk my car to the curb and sprint toward the shattered remains of Lauren's car...

- A young mother is distraught. Her small child is hospitalized with a terminal form of spinal meningitis and is not responding to treatment. My brother, a friend, and I do our best to comfort the mother with scripture, then lay hands on her daughter, praying for a miracle.

- The recession of 2007 has undermined my financial support base, revealing both the vulnerability of the ministry I'm in and the inadequacy of my support strategy. An entirely new approach must be innovated and implemented without delay. A colleague shares an idea, and I leap to give it a shot.

- After decades of success, the ministry team on which I serve realizes that our primary strategy is no longer functional. Immense structural changes have taken place in the marketplace. Our delivery system and process must be scrapped and replaced by something far more responsive, nimble, and accessible. We roll up our sleeves, pray, and innovate a radical new design requiring a full year of R&D.

- I'm shocked to learn that a large sum of money is missing from a capital campaign. The only person with access to the funds is a nationally respected executive with whom I'm scheduled to meet in the next few minutes. If the conversation doesn't go well, it could undermine my career. I go and raise the concern head-on.

- I've been involved in an awful automobile accident. Months later we've learned that the police report has been falsified and the judge has been manipulated to rule against me. Approaching the sentencing hearing my attorney and I have labored to craft a carefully-worded defense of my role in the tragedy. On the way to court, the Lord instructs me to remove from my prepared remarks *every argument* to defend myself. Having redacted almost everything from my script, I stand before the judge and face my accusers.

- A ministry to which I'm committed is facing financial hardship that can be assuaged by a risky real estate purchase. After prayer, I enroll two friends and we make the complicated transaction anonymously.

- While praying, I'm impressed by God (I think) to "deliver a message" to the Mayor. For the next several days, I strive to dismiss the thought as a ridiculous concoction of my overactive imagination. The longer I struggle, the stronger the conviction that I'm to make an appointment, sit down with the Mayor, and ask him a very specific question about his relationship with God. I make the appointment, meet with the Mayor, and ask the question.

Each of these scenarios challenged my willingness to trust the Lord. Many times I wrestled with God: "Did I hear you right?" or "Are you *sure* this is what you want me to do?" or "Oh God, help!"

At times I was nearly paralyzed by rational and irrational fears. Through each adventure, God's goodness, God's faithfulness, and God's sovereignty became paramount. The promise in Romans 8:28 has been my touchstone: "And we know that all things work together for good to those who love God and are called according to His purpose." Armed with the confidence that "God has me, God has us, and God has this," I leapt into uncharted waters, clinging to Jesus.

Like me, you have had many adventures with God. Moments in your life when only God could rescue you, where you absolutely needed God's intervention to keep you aright. I invite you, right now, to take several minutes to journal at least a dozen examples of your own Adventurous Life with Jesus.

Paul says that he *pressed on to take hold of that for which Christ Jesus took hold of him.* [Philippians 3:12] This "pressing on" suggests an ardor so intense, a struggle so severe, an exertion so demanding as to have required *his all.* I wonder if our pursuit of Christ's calling to change our world would blanche in comparison with that of Paul.

Writing to the Church at Ephesus, about the ferocity of the spiritual struggle that is the Christian life, Paul penned: *"...and after you have done everything, to stand. Stand..."* [Ephesians 6:13b-14a] I understand this to mean: "after you've given *everything* in you to stand, keep standing!"

My friend Ennio Salucci has, for almost twenty years, championed me to live a life of bold, decisive action. He says it this way: *Throw your body into the middle of the room, and see what God does with it!*

So many times since then when I've been facing threatening and complex problems that I have no wisdom, experience, or ability to adequately address, *I coach myself:* "Throw your body into the middle of the room, Kirk, and see what God does with it!" I picture myself grabbing myself by the scruff of my neck, and tossing my body into the middle of the mess. Right into the midst of the chaos. THERE, I'm confident I'll find Jesus waiting for me.

Notice, he's not here on the sidelines. No, Jesus is *there*, in the muck and mire waiting for me to arrive. He's ready to show himself strong on my behalf. [2 Chronicles 16:9]

To *fully participate* in the life God has given us, knowing that in ourselves we're not enough, is to apprehend the adventurous life.

See you there!

For Personal Reflection:

The Church today seems to have so little tolerance for the possibility of failure, loss, or harm that it's unwilling to engage in *any* adventure. This reality is *stunning* in light of the Biblical record. In it, the Christian life is portrayed as *anything* but safe, cautious, predictable, measured, and reasonable. Everywhere in the Bible, those who followed God were *adventurers*.

- Compare how you've led your organization through the most recent three years to the risks you took your first three years.

- What did your example of risk and adventure produce in those you influenced in those early years?

- What effect has your more recent example of calculated planning and minimized risk had on those you try to influence?

- If "ministry flows out of being," what has become of your courageous willingness to trust Christ with your whole being?

For Group Discussion:

- How frequently does your organization invite followers into the *adventure* of following Jesus?

- How often do you remind those you influence that challenges beyond the believer's ability are a *completely normal* part of the Christian lifestyle?

- As those you influence encounter hardships, what has your practice been? Are you more likely to call them to pursue Christ, or do you move to undo the difficulty they're experiencing?

- Discuss what you have seen produced in the community or organization when each of these strategies is employed.

CHAPTER 11

Undermine the 80/20 Rule

Why is it that 20% of the people in our churches are doing virtually all the giving, all the serving, and all the ministry?

What if we who lead have actually established the culture that reinforces the 80/20 rule?

What are we communicating such that the vast majority of church attenders feel great about coming, taking, and *contributing nothing*?

And, though you're unaware of it, pastor, what if *this is exactly what you want*?

I invite you to ponder: what are you doing to perpetuate 80/20 in your congregation?

Since, according to Edwin Friedman "No one has ever gone from slavery to freedom with the slaveholders cheering them on," I fully expect to encounter your resistance to this claim: 80/20 is yet another evidence of *the culture of cowardice* that is alive and well in much of the American Church.

Take a breath. Set your resistance aside, and gather your key leaders. Lock yourselves in a conference room until you can identify at least ten ways your church communications, culture, and leadership promote and preserve 80/20.

Think about it.

One: What do we model when, every time the doors are open, a relative handful minister to the many who simply spectate?

When a thousand gather for "worship" what do they see?

One preaches. Another does announcements. One or two run the soundboard, show the videos, dim the lights. Maybe a dozen play instruments or sing in a worship band. Or, maybe you have an organist. *One* organist and a soloist. A couple dozen function as greeters and ushers. And, several dozen teach the children, but that happens elsewhere – out of sight of most of the adults.

What you model reinforces a culture in which very few do a great deal and very many do almost nothing.

Don't they?

Your denominational polity may require that only a select few minister to the many who gather. If it is, my invitation is to innovate ways outside your formal service where many in the laity can learn to minister the goodness of God.

Two: What expectations are communicated to those who gather at your weekend services?

Park here. Don't smoke in the building. Sign in your kids. Leave your coffee outside the sanctuary. Give, if you're comfortable. Take part in this class, that event, the other small group experience. *Please come back!*

You can boil down the "contract" you make with your folks this way: "Just come back; we'll take care of everything."

If they do return, they do exactly what you've asked: *nothing.* Usually, this goes on for years.

Three: How frequently and how clearly do you teach your congregation about giving?

Funny, isn't it? Jesus spoke *more* about money than any subject other than the Kingdom of God.

Why?

Because what I treasure reveals my heart. [Matthew 6:21] Yet, most pastors *dread* speaking about finances. "People will think that *all* we care about is money" some of you say. So, you rarely teach the topic and how closely allied it is to *all* issues of the heart of your people…and yet *you think about money all the time.*

Don't you?

See, if you're in the business of packing pews (what I call *"the religious education and entertainment business"*) you'll avoid all the topics that invite people to take offense.

These are the same topics that reveal what people truly value.

Isn't it strange that Jesus wasn't smart enough to remember this, since he addressed the topic of money so very, very often? In fact, if you study his behavior, you'll conclude that keeping the crowds coming back wasn't nearly as important to Jesus as it is to us.

What *was* Jesus' priority?

Why did Jesus say what he said?

Why did he teach what he did, tell the stories he told, and live among people the way he did?

I assert that Jesus was in the people-development business. Jesus was making *Kingdom citizens* of people. And, when it happened, those people lived in *very* distinct ways.

"Discipleship," to Jesus, had everything to do with *how people live*, and *why* they do what they do. He was laser-focused on the heart-posture and motivation behind people's actions. Discipleship began with the renovation of the heart; a heart-posture that expresses itself in a way-of-being in the world that is remarkable. [Acts 16:7]

Yet, in North America, church members' way-of-being in society seems *anything but remarkable.*

Doesn't it?

Ever wondered how cults are successful getting a following despite their whacky teaching and bizarre priorities?

One reason is that they communicate *clear and challenging expectations* to their followers. Often, these are very rigorous requirements. Though the cults' demands are frequently misguided and always theologically corrupt, people by the thousands "pony up" whatever is required.

Maybe the cult leaders *abuse* the scriptures that you *avoid?*

Still, Jesus said: *"If anyone will come after me, he (or she) must take up their cross daily and follow me."* [Matthew 16:24, Mark 8:34] Yet, such preaching is rarely heard in the namby-pamby, keep-them-coming-back Church of our day.

I wonder what prices we pay as a result. *I wonder what prices America is paying.* Don't you?

How to Undermine 80/20

As senior pastor, elder, or lay leader, what can you do to *undermine the 80/20 Rule* in your congregation?

One: Think like a people-developer, not a gatherer of spectators.

Re-think why you're in Christian ministry.

Decide to jettison the notion, promoted by almost three hundred years of post-enlightenment Church culture, that your role *primarily* is to educate and entertain church people.

Instead, become *primarily* a disciple-maker and maturity-provoker. When your purpose is to catalyze people to live like Jesus, so much of the activity that fills and frustrates your workweek will change.

Think about it.

What if your senior staff took 80% of the hours it devotes to preparing for and pulling off a slick service—an education and entertainment event—and dedicated that time to imagining ways to provoke Christ-likeness in your people?

What if you became *trainers, coaches, and equippers* rather than event planners and show producers?

What *experiences* would support your people's growth into maturity?

- What skills would you *be sure* to have them <u>practice</u>? Perhaps you could give them drills in discerning God's direction, praying for others effectively, and listening well?

- What would you have them <u>role play</u>? Perhaps, you could instruct them to communicate parts of their Christ-story so as to connect with a variety of people in any number of life situations, to respond biblically to universal ethical and moral challenges, and to select appropriate scriptures that could support people facing common difficulties, life experiences, and perplexities?

- What <u>field trip</u> experiences would be core to your disciple-making process? How could you have your people serve those outside the church who are culturally similar to them, volunteer with secular service organizations, and interview civic leaders [police officials, Mayor's office, school administrators, YWCA director, city council members] about the true needs of neighboring residents?

- How would you ensure that your people <u>applied</u> what you teach them when you do an education event? What pathways can you pave *in advance* of your weekend education events so that every person can take action in line with their new learning?

<u>Two:</u> Stop counting the numbers of spectators who amass at your weekend events. Instead, fix your staff's attention on those who are making a difference for Christ: those who are serving, contributing, ministering. Rivet your collective leadership attention *here.*

Decide what maturing in Christ looks like in your context. Is it serving the unchurched by giving sacrificially of one's money, time, and talents? Count those who live *this way.* It is those who contribute, who serve, and who minister outside as well as inside the church who most likely are maturing as Christ-like disciples.

Count *only* these!

Focus on *their* progress. Use *them* as examples when you teach and train. Make *them* your congregation's visible heroes.

Pay attention to their growth. Who among them is *God* stretching, growing, maturing, and strengthening?

What are the experiences that seem to contribute to the development of their character, confidence in ministry, trust in Christ, and tenderness of heart?

What can you, as a senior leadership team do to provoke your people to love and to do good works? [Hebrews 10:24]

While you're doing that, wean yourself off your fixation with *how many attend* this or that. To undermine the 80/20 rule, stop yourself from caring about how many come and listen. Stop asking about how many simply sit and take and leave.

Three: Innovate ways to involve everyone, every time. A *lot* of people come to the church Annie and I attend. What if, routinely in our services, we grouped people and asked them to find someone in the group with whom they discover they have something in common, then turn that common ground into prayer?

What if our greeters grabbed the first ten strangers who walked in, and asked them to help greet our guests?

What if our ushers randomly asked people to help them?

What if our trained prayer team picked a handful of people to whom they gave *one minute* of prayer training, then had them come alongside and assist when praying for others?

What if every ministry team, the weekend before they do some local ministry, randomly asked people in the service to come and do it with them? What if they kept asking until 15 people agreed to come and help?

What if you made it clear that your church is a community where, from day one, *everyone gives.*

Where *everyone contributes.* Where *everyone plays.*

What if giving, contributing, and playing is actually how mature disciples are made?

Is it "Grace?"

Could it be that a distorted substitute for biblical grace has taken the Church? Consider how little the Church asks of Christians—in the name of "grace."

Consider the abundance of resources we make available *to Christians* who are expected to contribute nothing in return. Churches, in general, are so transfixed with providing for their own that they have little time, energy, and resources with which to serve the unchurched.

Think about how much time and energy the Church spends on <u>itself</u>:

Baby dedications	Baptisms
Child care	Moms' nights out
Children's ministry	Men's breakfasts
Youth group	Relationship counseling
Women's teas	Extravagant holiday productions
College and career ministry	Pre-marital classes
Weddings	Marriage counseling
Divorce recovery	Grief counseling
Financial management seminars	Debt counseling

Bereavement care	Memorial services

Our churches provide cradle-to-grave services to the saved—most of which are free of any call that the recipients contribute to the community of faith from which they take, take, and take. My point is not whether these activities should occur. Their inclusion illustrates the abundance of free services churches provide to Christians (who feel entitled to them). These commitments leave few resources to actually grow Christians up and demonstrate the good news to those who don't yet know Christ.

Is it any wonder that fewer than 10% of church-attenders tithe?

Have you ever been a part of a church during a major capital campaign? What happened?

For a capital campaign to succeed, two things have to occur: those who already give must dig deep and give more, usually *a lot* more, and they often do. And also, those who rarely give and those who only *gesture at giving* are called upon to sacrifice as well. That's where the commotion commences, doesn't it?

A capital campaign—like the claims of Lordship that Jesus so clearly articulates—calls each of us to painful sacrifice. In Matthew 10:38, Mark 8:34, Luke 9:23 and 14:27 the Gospels record Jesus' clearly: *"If anyone would come after me, he must deny himself and take up his cross daily and follow me."*

Yet, in our commitment to be visitor-sensitive, we communicate in dozens of ways that cross-bearing is optional. It is not expected and certainly not insisted upon. Then, when we finally call our people—all of them—to get into the game in a sacrificial way, many of them pack up and leave for another church or no church at all.

Don't they?

Look at what all this visitor-sensitivity has produced. Do you see maturing disciples all around you?

Do you?

A number of years ago *Habitat for Humanity* approved my friends Richard and Jackie Higley for a Habitat house. Working the graveyard shift in a manufacturing plant, driving a cab, and doing odd jobs whenever he could still wouldn't provide the down payment my buddy would need to own a home.

Habitat, however, has a pathway to home ownership.

Richard and Jackie donated their time, lots of it, to help other *Habitat* recipients build their homes over a number of years. When the time came to work on *their* home, dozens of others were there to help out.

Many of us who love them pitched in as well.

It was a blast. Rewarding. Resourceful. Empowering. Richard and Jackie had "skin in the game." They got far more than a home. They invested themselves in their home in a way that changed them.

Why doesn't *Habitat* just hand out homes? They could. They could use a lottery system to select the fortunate few who'd get a nice new *Habitat* house for free. But they don't.

Know why?

Because, getting a house for free doesn't mature people.

It doesn't develop character. It doesn't strengthen confidence. It doesn't shift one's self-perception like it did for Richard and Jackie.

Pastor, if you're in the disciple-making business then you're in the business of changing people. You're to be changing people into the image of Christ, God's Spirit working with you. You're to regularly be provoking people to live and love and give and care and serve the way Jesus did—motivated by what motivated him.

That rarely happens when you keep handing people fish.

Back in Chapter 8, I told you about how I was struggling my way through a character-development workshop in Honolulu with Dan, my trainer and mentor. Dan's life-changing counsel was this:

Kirk, we're not here to give people fish. We're not here to teach them to fish.

We're here to provoke their hunger!

Are you?

FOR PERSONAL REFLECTION:

A capital campaign, like the claims of Lordship that Jesus so clearly articulates, calls each of us to painful sacrifice. Jesus is clear: *"If anyone would come after me, he must deny himself and take up his cross daily and follow me."* In our commitment to being visitor-sensitive, we communicate in dozens of ways that cross-bearing is optional, not expected, and certainly not insisted upon. When we finally call our people into the game in a sacrificial way, many of them pack up and leave.

- When you consider how much harder we work than Jesus did to shelter people from his claims of Lordship on their lives what do we produce?
- List five major prices the Church pays.
- List five major payoffs (i.e., actual benefits), you as a leader, receive.
- How might your last capital campaign have been different had you been clearly calling all your people to sacrificial commitment for the years leading up to it?
- How would *you* have been different?

FOR GROUP DISCUSSION:

What if your senior staff took 80% of the hours it devotes to planning, preparing, and pulling off your weekend services and dedicated that time to imagining ways to provoke Christ-likeness in your people, becoming *trainers, coaches, and equippers* rather than event planners and show producers? Collaborate to select three answers to each of these questions:

- What *experiences* would support your people's growth into maturity?
- What *skills* would you be sure to have them practice?

- What would you have them *role play*?
- What *field trips* would be core to your disciple-making process?
- How could you have them *serve outside* the church?

CHAPTER 12

The Unreasonableness of Being Reasonable

We're looking at Christian leadership from what I hope are refreshing and resourceful perspectives. I am indebted to Edwin Friedman for sparking these thoughts with his charge to *"disengage from an unreasonable faith in reasonableness."*

Pastor, after all the years of disappointments, setbacks, and betrayals in your experience as both minister and disciple, have you become reasoned, balanced, measured, and composed in the application of your faith?

Has your Christianity become, somehow, affordable?

I wonder how this impacts those you seem unable to inspire. We are, after all, talking about leading with courage.

If the Christian faith is but one among many, then a sensibly reasonable approach to applying its teachings is appropriate. If Christianity is just one philosophy among several, holding your faith as you do your political convictions is understandable. If church involvement is considered one of numerous "membership commitments" then it is wise to be measured in your investment.

The thing is, *Christianity cannot be any of these, for any of us.* If it is but one of many of *anything*, then it is a lie.

A hoax.

The reasonable thing to do is to have nothing to do with it.

The claims of Christ are so radical, singular, and exclusive they stand alone. Without rival in all of human history. They should be unrivaled in our lives.

So, the seminal question: *Is Christianity true?*

If Jesus Christ is the completely unique Son of God [John 3:16], the way, the truth, and the life, the only route to the Father [John 14:6], the One in whom the fullness of God dwells [Colossians 2:9], then to be reasonable in your commitment to your faith is the most unreasonable thing you could ever do.

To be reasonable in your commitment to Christ is the most unreasonable thing you could ever do. And to be unreasonable in your commitment to Jesus and His Church is the most reasonable thing you could ever do.

No *reasonable* person can declare "For me to live is Christ and to die is gain." [Philippians 1:21] Right?

Maybe you rationalize: "That was Paul. *The Apostle* Paul. Heck, he wrote half the New Testament. Paul's was a highly unusual commitment to Christ and Christianity."

Yet, Paul was crazy or he *fully* expected the Christians in Philippi to do the same thing with their lives that he did.

Didn't he?

Paul, like Jesus, was no reasonable person.

Gripped at his core, from his core, to his core with the unreasonableness of faith, everything Paul wrote and modeled indicated a radical, all-in embrace of faith.

All-in. Are you?

A LESSON FROM CHURCHILL

It seems that the Church in North America is reasonable if it is anything, and that reasonableness has got us stuck.

"Syncretism" is what scholars call it. The term refers to the unnatural amalgamation of different religions, cultures, or schools of thought. The result is the loss of what made each distinctive (and valuable).

I call it a blight that is foundational to the culture of cowardice that's become commonplace in the Church today. One way to regain our verve is to take an axe to the roots of the commitment to be reasonable.

Trouble is, there's *comfort* in reasonableness. You can find a degree of *security* there, too. The moderation it provokes can masquerade as *wisdom* after you've had any number of flameouts when taking bold steps of faith.

As a new Christian, I had the unfortunate experience of being discipled in a church that regularly twisted scripture and abused power. Over time, many people were scarred emotionally and spiritually. Hundreds never recovered.

A decade later, Annie and I invested ourselves—without reservation—in a church plant that imploded after two leaders had an extra-marital affair. In hindsight, all the indications were there. Annie and I hadn't seen the affair taking shape, but we could have. The ripple effects were devastating—particularly for those new to Christ.

Years later we gave what *for us* was a breathtaking sum of money for a capital campaign. Then we learned that a person on the inside had misappropriated tens of thousands from that campaign.

Sad.

If you've been around the Church for any time, scandals are nothing new. How the perpetrators can sleep at night is incomprehensible to me. What is not mysterious is the pressure these setbacks have exerted on my enthusiasm to live "all-in" for Christ. It's as if powerful spiritual forces conspire to soften my commitment to live boldly for Christ.

They do.

A "voice of reason" resonates in my head coaxing me to be moderate. One prevailing paradigm suggests that we hold our faith as we would a country club membership or allegiance to an alma mater: one of many commitments. Important maybe, but not essential and certainly nothing to lose your head over.

In the scriptures, moderation in living for Christ is never esteemed.

Who are the heroes of moderation?

Peter in Caiaphas' courtyard. Thomas, in disbelief. Judas Iscariot.

Jesus is unambiguous: Whoever wants to be my disciple must deny themselves and take up their cross daily and follow me. [Luke 9:23]

Clear as a bell.

No one can serve two masters. Either you will hate the one and love the other. [Luke 16:13]

As a leader, who you are is more important than anything you say. In fact, who you are is more important than everything you say.

Some ministers are master pulpiteers. Skilled rhetoricians. Gifted orators. Big talkers.

Talk that's not backed by a consistent life has a hollow ring, and that hollowness drives people away—away from church and away from *the* Church.

When Winston Churchill addressed the Harrow School in late October 1941 his speech included these most famous words: "Never give in. Never give in. Never, never, never, never—in nothing, great or small, large or petty—never give in, except to convictions of honor and good sense. Never yield to force. Never yield to the apparently overwhelming might of the enemy."

His words, then and now, ring true. You know why?

Because <u>Churchill</u> *didn't give in.*

Neville Chamberlain, the British Prime Minister prior to Churchill, was known as the "great appeaser" who capitulated to Adolf Hitler. Chamberlain could never have made that speech. If he had, it would not have been remembered.

The words didn't match his life.

Do yours?

WHO YOU ARE

Pastor, *who you are,* is more important than anything you say.

In fact, who you are is more important than <u>everything</u> you say!

This book is a call to the courageous, risky life that leaders lived in the Church of the New Testament. It stands in glaring contrast to the lifestyle of the professional clergy that, more often than not, resembles tenured professors at our nation's universities, without the taxpayer-funded salary package.

This is primarily troubling because you are not primarily an educator... you are a role model.

Just like Timothy, Deborah, Paul, Priscilla & Aquila, Barnabas, Esther, John, and Stephen. Yes, *just like* them.

If not you, then who?

Who else is to model the vibrant, sold-out Christian life than you and your elders?

Those who write books, like those who traverse the Christian speaking circuit, don't provide the regular proximity and access that you, as shepherd of a local congregation, do—unless you hide in your study and only emerge when it's time to preach or take charge of a meeting.

Think about those words: proximity and access.

If the lyrics and music of your preaching and your life don't align, those words will strike fear in you.

If, however, you've raised your way-of-living to match your preaching or aligned your preaching to that which you actually live, those words will resonate with your heart.

When your life is "Chamberlainian," the dissonance between your life and the biblical message undercuts your effectiveness as a leader of God's women and men. When your living is "Churchillian" the bravery to which you call your congregation will remind them of the courage they see you routinely summon to bring God's reign to the chaos and disorder that has besieged your community.

One of my favorite preachers is Mike Erre. Mike's always been an amazing Bible expositor and communicator. Biblically-sound. Funny. Profound. Engaging.

Illuminating. Winsome.

In recent years, a medical crisis has befallen someone *very* dear to Mike and Justina. A crisis from which there's no apparent recovery. Since the crisis, Mike's preaching has gained *gravitas*, like Jesus when the scholars marveled at his understanding [Luke 2:47] and demons quaked in his presence [Mark 5:7]. *You can sense it* when you're around Mike. This man knows what it is to follow Jesus *no matter what.*

When you live in harmony with the Biblical message, you have gravitas. Weight.

Substance. Authenticity.

So does your preaching.

When you don't live your message, your sermons are hollow. That hollowness drives folks away. The first to go are the true believers. The uncompromising. The bold. The spirited. The gutsy. The ones who read their Bibles and believe it says what it says and it means what it means. These are the people who long for authenticity. Not theory. They want to associate with a faith community that will *live* this stuff—Jesus' stuff—like it's real.

Because it is. It is.

What our Values Communicate

Reasonable leadership is *ruining* the Church in North America in our time.

We've pointed out that when you preach what you don't practice, the dissonance repels people—not just from your sanctuary—but from Christianity. The implications for society are deeply profound and can infect it for generations.

Christianity is nothing if not a call to courage. When her leaders bow before the idol of reasonableness, a dry, hum-drum philosophical religion results.

And, men leave the church in droves. Or haven't you noticed?

I subscribe to an excellent service called *Leader's Book Summaries* [www.StudyLeadership.com]. I *highly* recommend it. In a summary of David Murrow's *Why Men Hate Going to Church* I learned that only one third of church attendees are men—and most of them are over 60. It's almost impossible to find adults of either gender under age 40 in church.

How come?

Consider these two lists of values.

First, the bolded list: **Love, communication, beauty, relationships, support, help, nurture, feelings, sharing, harmony, community, and cooperation.**

And, the italicized list: *Competence, power, efficiency, achievement, skills, results, accomplishment, technology, goals, success, and competition.*

Which list of values do you think is most consistent with the culture that predominates the North American Church today?

The bold list or *the italicized list?*

Both lists come from John Gray's *Men are from Mars, Women are from Venus* and they distinguish culturally "masculine" and "feminine" values.

What do you see?

In our commitment to be reasonable, I suggest that the Church in the West has been emasculated. Neutered. Actually, in my view, it's been feminized.

Consider this: those most absent from church are men and young adults.

According to Murrow, they esteem challenge over security. The key values of this missing population include: adventure, risk, daring, independence, variety, and reward.

Women and seniors are more likely to embrace as core values: safety, stability, harmony, predictability, comfort, support, and tradition.

Since values are revealed in behavior, what does *your* lifestyle disclose, pastor? When the time has come to take a courageous stand, what does *your* behavior reveal?

- When the opportunity came to stand up to that manipulative, obstructionist power-wielding elder, what did you do?
- When you thought to lead your parish out into the city to serve, love, and impact those outside your tight-knit congregation—and pushback came, *as it always does*—did you lead courageously or cave under pressure?
- When a clear biblical injunction has become as unpopular in your denomination as in the culture at large, have you censored your own voice?
- When the Holy Spirit stirred you to put your hand to the plow in pursuit of some great, challenging work for God's glory, did the fearful complaints of the cowardly prevail in the end?

As leaders, we get to champion our people to become who they always wanted to be, by taking them where they never wanted to go.

And, since life is always lived from now on, your past behavior is no predictor of the greatness you'll accomplish before you breathe your last.

So, before you see Jesus face to face, what great, rewarding, daring adventure will you and your people give yourselves to?

What'll it be?

You get to choose.

For Personal Reflection:

When your living is "Churchillian," the bravery to which you call your congregation will remind them of the courage they see you routinely summon to bring God's reign to the chaos and disorder that has besieged your community.

- Identify four instances when you called those you influence "to bravery."
- Why was bravery needed?
- How rare is it for you to "summon courage to bring God's reign to the chaos and disorder that has besieged your community?"
- When is the most recent time those you lead could say they've seen you being courageous?
- Over the next twelve months, determine three opportunities you see to bring God's reign into some area of brokenness or pain. Determine to be an example of courage *in full view* of your people. What will you do? How will anyone know?

For Group Discussion:

When you live in harmony with the Biblical message, the author says you have gravitas. Weight. Substance. Authenticity. And, so does your preaching. When you don't live your message, your sermons are hollow. That hollowness drives folks away. Some of the first to go are the true believers. The uncompromising. The bold. The spirited. The gutsy. The ones who read their Bibles and believe it says what it says and it means what it means. These are the people who long for authenticity, who want to associate with a faith community that will *live* Jesus' stuff like it's real. Because it is.

- Describe what it was like if ever you've been connected to a faith community that lived the message they proclaimed with uncompromising authenticity.

- Who is someone you know who speaks with the "gravitas" described in this chapter?

- What factors have contributed to her or his weightiness?

- Discuss the degree to which your faith community currently lives "Jesus' stuff" like it's real. What are the greatest gaps between proclamation and application?

- What contributes most to and detracts most from your community living Jesus' message and lifestyle?

CHAPTER 13

Go First!

Could you imagine the impact of a largely *leaderless Church* in the United States for, say, two hundred years?

Well, look around...

We're heading into the home stretch on this examination of courageous Christian leadership. Thus far, we've made eight observations about leadership in a culture of cowardice:

One: *Courageous leadership is not about skill, technique, or knowledge. It is, most of all, about the presence of the leader as he or she moves through life.*

Two: *Take full responsibility for your own emotional being and destiny.*

Three: *Promote healthy differentiation within the church or system you lead.*

Four: *Stand, as an exemplar, in the sabotage and backlash that must come.*

Five: *Don't "push on the rope:" the unmotivated are invulnerable to insight.*

Six: *Undermine the 80/20 Rule.*

Seven: *Reintroduce yourself to the adventurous life.*

Eight: *Disengage an unreasonable faith in reasonableness.*

This brings us to the ninth principle: *Go first.*

Ever wonder what happened to the Church the Apostle Paul envisioned in Ephesians chapter four; a Church in which the saints are the "ministers?"

Paul is clear: *Christ himself gave* the apostles, the prophets, the evangelists, the pastors and teachers, *to equip his people* for works of service, so that the body of Christ may be built up… and become mature… Then we will no longer be infants… Instead… we will grow to become in every respect the mature body… the whole body… grows and builds itself up in love, as each part does its work. [Ephesians 4:11-16]

In Paul's conception, Christ gives ministers to the church to train, develop, and equip the members to minister, to mature in every respect, and to w-o-r-k.

Question: What has dominated the practice and priorities of Christian leadership, almost universally, since the Reformation?

Answer: Religious educators who teach and teach and teach the saints who sit and sit and sit while they learn and learn and learn.

Question: What's missing?

Answer: The saints ministering. The body maturing. Every part working.

Now here's a shock. What if the culprit is not so much the lethargy of the saints but the focus and function of the clergy?

See, Christ himself gave apostolic, prophetic, evangelistic, pastoral, and teaching gifts to equip his Church for maturity and ministry.

Yet, since the Enlightenment, seminary is the route to ministry for most. What do our seminaries produce? The answer is an overwhelming super-abundance of pastor-teachers.

Period.

Imagine a softball team in which catchers play all nine positions. Very well-equipped catchers. Maybe overly well-equipped catchers.

Can you see it?

Catcher's glove. Catcher's mask. Chest protector. Shin pads. The whole get-up.

Now, put that catcher on the mound and ask her to pitch... Put her in left to run down a deep fly ball... Or, at short to turn a ground ball into a double play.

This is the Church in the West today.

What do teaching-gifted ministers produce? They produce people who learn. People who learn lots of things, *important things,* and not much else. *I'm not denigrating the teaching gift. I'm denigrating the notion of the teaching-only ministry.* I'm inviting *you* to look at the results of recurring generations of pastor/teacher-dominant ministry in the West.

Are you impressed by what *you* see?

THE APOSTOLIC GRACE

What do you miss when apostolic grace is missing from the Church?

An apostle is a "sent-one." Walk into the dozen churches closest to your home and send the members out into the community to minister there. Call them to establish the Kingdom reign and rule of God out there. Challenge them to pioneer fresh and meaningful expressions of ministry that make sense to the prevailing culture—outside their walls.

The Christians in those churches will look at you like you're insane! The longer they've been "churched" the more aghast they will be. If they've been attending church their entire lives, their incredulity will be nearly insurmountable.

Why?

The religious culture in which they've been steeped has trained them to be scandalized by the assertion that they're supposed to minister regularly, routinely, naturally, and passionately among those who are not followers of the Christian way. Church culture has taught them to believe that's what ministers are paid for. "It is the minister's job to minister. Our job is to come and sit and listen and *sort of* tithe."

Trust me on this.

I'm close to a few Senior Pastors who challenged their people in just this way—and the power brokers who control their elder boards ran the pastors out. Out of the church. Out of town. Out of pastoral ministry.

They argued that church resources shouldn't be squandered on those in the community outside. The pastors' time, church facilities, and its finances are to be reserved for the care and comfort of church members. To suggest that pastors would have the audacity to minister to the lost, to those *outside* the body, and to train and lead the congregation to do the same was so disgraceful that the pastors had to be removed, and they were!

A tragedy.

It is heartbreaking for the pastors. It's far more disastrous for the congregations left behind, mired in meaningless maintenance of impotent programs and life-sapping control. *The greatest catastrophe, however, is for those the Church continues to ignore,* insulating them from what would have been provocative demonstrations of Christ's transformative presence in their midst.

They just go to Hell.

Does this remind you, at all, of Jesus' words: *"What sorrow awaits you teachers of religious law and you Pharisees. Hypocrites! For you shut the door of the Kingdom of Heaven in people's faces. You won't go in yourselves, and you don't let others enter either.* [Matthew 23:13 NLT]

See, the apostolic impetus ignites action. It generates groundbreaking innovation. It leads change. It is consumed with whatever could expand the reach and impact of the Kingdom of God. The apostolic is risk-taking, not safety-centered. Its orientation is forward.

Forward looking. Forward leaning. Forward moving.

Teaching is valuable in so much as it produces Christ-honoring Kingdom advance in individuals, in congregations, and in society.

Christ gave the apostolic to the Church for its effectiveness.

Where the apostolic is missing, minimized, or marginalized, you get, well… you get what we have today.

THE PROPHETIC GRACE

We're looking at a ninth characteristic of courageous Christian leadership. A leader moves. She takes action. *Rather than conducting a straw poll to see what the prevailing opinions are, a leader will go first,* and sometimes this means going alone for a while.

It's nothing special. It's what *leaders* do.

As we investigate going first, we're reminded that Christ gave three distinct ministry gifts to the church: apostle, prophet, and evangelist to compliment that of the pastor-teacher [Ephesians 4:11]. Yet, since the Reformation, pastor-teachers have been leading, largely, in a vacuum. *The over emphasis on shepherding and teaching has produced both the Church and the society that we have today.*

Going first includes restoring the apostolic, prophetic, and evangelistic graces to Christian leadership.

What becomes of the Church when the prophetic is marginalized?

You get an indistinct, mushy, shallow, and disingenuously "nice" message week after week. The trumpet blows a vague, indistinguishable, uncertain sound. [I Corinthians 14:8]

Where there's no prophetic voice, there's no distinctively Christian lifestyle either. Sin can thrive in an atmosphere like that.

And, it does. Doesn't it?

The prophetic grace brings clarity when the church and its leaders wobble and wander. The prophetic brings courageous correction. It is the scalpel that cuts between the diseased and the healthy tissue around it. It provides a clear word from God (or from God's Word) when the Church is blurring the lines of biblical acuity.

Think about Nathan's role in the life of King David [2 Samuel 12:1-14]. Where might David's arrogance, selfishness, and entitlement have taken him were it not for the timeliness, the clarity, and the strength of the prophet's rebuke?

When you mix the kind of power that many ministry leaders have with their human frailty disaster often results. When it does, innocents are hurt and the veracity of the Christian faith is undermined.

What if the prophetic voice was just as visible, authoritative, and influential in the Church in North America as the pastor-teacher's voice has been? Imagine if they stood side-by-side to mature the Church and to improve her efficacy in society.

Which of the high-profile scandals that have rocked the Christian Church could have been avoided?

More imperative, how much more mature, godly, and authentically *Christian* might the Church be today?

Allow yourself to consider the moral, spiritual, and ethical condition of American society if the prophetic had been as influential as the shepherd-teacher has for the last couple hundred years.

"Christ gave some to be apostles and some to be prophets."

Since Christ has given them to the Church, don't you wonder where they are?

THE EVANGELISTIC GRACE

We're considering the ninth characteristic of those who would lead well in a culture overrun with cowardice. Early in the book we examined why comfort-craving, security-seeking, spiritless stagnation is common in the Church. Sad, when you consider how Christians behaved in the Book of Acts.

Isn't it?

Christ gave apostles, prophets, evangelists, pastors and teachers to equip the saints for the work of their ministry. [Ephesians 4:11-16] Do you find it strange that for several generations there's been almost no evidence of the first three of these essential graces in the North American Church?

One quality of "going first" is to restore these missing graces to our churches. What is the impact on the Church when the evangelistic impetus is in scant supply? Seriously, look around.

Because of the preponderance of the teaching grace, you get a dysfunctional over-emphasis on *teaching as the means of evangelism.*

Whenever you are with anyone, you create an experience with that person. When you keep trying to teach those who are not postured to learn, what do *they* experience?

I compare it to scratching someone where they *don't* have an itch. It is irritating. Trying to teach those who don't want to learn creates the experience of annoyance, condescension, and frustration.

This we do in the name of Jesus.

The second thing you get with an overemphasis on the teaching gift is a scarcity of actual "evangels." At the heart of the word "evangelism" is "angel." An angel is a messenger.

An "ev-angel" is a messenger of good, and a message is "good" when those who receive it define it that way.

Think about it.

Recall the angels' message at the first advent? Was it: "Turn or burn!" "Close this clinic!" "Vote for our candidate!" "Give up your lifestyle!" No, the angels' message was a proclamation:

"Do not be afraid. I bring you good news that will cause great joy for all the people. Today...a Savior has been born to you; he is the Messiah... Glory to God...and on earth peace to those on whom his favor rests." [Luke 2:11-14]

However, that message might be interpreted today, *it meant something really good* to the Hebrew people enslaved by Roman oppression in that hour.

Our society thinks it has heard our "evangel" and they've judged it as anything but "good."

They think they've heard enough from us—people they've decided are rigid, judgmental, hypocritical bigots who oppose much of what is considered to be progressive and enlightened in culture. Since we've reduced Christian ministry to explanation and oration, we keep trying to *teach* them the right way to think, believe, and act.

Did Jesus do it this way?

Consider the *Campaign of Nain*, recorded in Luke 7:11-17. Jesus approaches the town and sees a funeral procession. A widow is broken over the death of her child and a lot of people are in despair.

What does Jesus do?

As he sizes up the situation, his heart goes out to her. He walks up, touches the casket, raises the boy to life, and hands him to his mother.

That's it!

No altar call.

No self-promotion.

No commercial about Sunday's meeting at 10:00am on Solomon's Colonnade. In fact, Jesus *doesn't tell them* to do anything. Jesus brings the Kingdom and because he does, people are blessed. He is a messenger of good. An "ev-angel."

And they all get it.

Their conclusion is stunning: "God has come to help his people." [Luke 7:16] Is that what people conclude when you and I come to town?

GOING FIRST

Edwin Friedman says, "To be a leader, one must both have and embody a vision of where one wants to go. It is not a matter of knowing or believing one is right; it is a matter of taking the first step."

Leaders go first.

They just do.

When they don't, they fail to lead.

You may be an educator, an encourager, a tactician, a chaplain, an historian, a counselor, an entertainer, a soother, a manager, or a caretaker, but that does not make you a *leader*. And, leadership is essential for the Church to be the Church.

If you watched the excellent HBO World War II miniseries *The Pacific* you've seen the difference between leaders and everyone else. One episode features the grisly beach landing by US Marines on Peleliu. Before the landing craft can unload a fresh batch of inexperienced soldiers they come under devastating fire. Marines are hit while still on the boats. Deafening planes strafe just overhead, bombs falling.

Bedlam!

Dizzying. Disorienting. Most of the GI's who survive long enough to reach the sand freeze in fear as mortars and bullets take down their companions. The wounded scream, some writhing, others whimpering.

Then, over the din of the guns and the bombs you hear just a few voices. They are clear, confident, urgent voices.

It is the officers, giving directions. Compared to the rookies, they seem unconcerned about their own safety. Their focus is not dodging bullets or ducking when a mortar shell explodes. Their focus is the mission.

They urge their marines to get up and move—in the face of fear. *"You want to live? Get off the beach and move!"*

Leaders lead by going first.

Politicians in our day are known to modify their message and methods based on polling data. Seems to me, their concern is not "what's right?" but "what'll work?" This is what passes for leadership in a culture of cowardice. Friedman, as noted earlier, has observed that American society has become obsessed with safety. And, as it has, our culture has become chronically anxious. We have lost our appetite for adventure.

Courageous leadership, in a context like this, is rare.

Consider how Jesus made decisions. Remember that glorious moment, I call the "sermon in the synagogue" when, after challenging the crowd to "eat his flesh" and "drink his blood," *many of his disciples* turned and no longer followed him? [John 6:66] Shaken, Jesus gathers his remaining disciples and negotiates new, more reasonable terms of followership.

Or does he?

When you read the text, you see that his concern is the mission: to prepare citizens for the Father's Kingdom. He could not have cared less about being popular, drawing a crowd, or entertaining the masses. No, that was not his focus. He lived for an "Audience of One," in every way. And, it affected his priorities, his behavior, his motivations, and his ethics.

Recently, the pastor and elders of a church in Virginia publicly apologized for mishandling sexual abuses perpetrated by a minister on their staff. Their attorneys and insurance carrier went nuts. Admit to anything and you open yourself to lawsuits…maybe dozens. It was a major national news story particularly because the leaders of that church *did lead* with integrity. They did what was right, because it was right, whether it worked or not. They led.

Or, as Friedman says: They took the first step.

Will you?

BECAUSE IT'S RIGHT

I used the phrase *"do what's right because it's right, whether it works or not."* I learned this from my dear friend, Tom, who says he learned it from the Lord. Through a series of sudden, unexpected, and unexplainable family tragedies, Tom found himself in isolation. Living alone, feverishly working two jobs, and cut off from those he loved most in the world, Tom had every incentive to be embittered and vindictive. Like most of us, he could've fought "fire with fire." Instead, he chose to do what's right because it's right, whether it worked or not. Whether he'd ever be restored to the rich relationships that were foundational to his life. He determined to love, serve, and support those who, through misunderstanding, had grown distrustful of him.

Leaders go first. Which means they GO. Leaders move into the unknown. They realize they cannot afford to wait until there's no risk left. *Guided by their values and attending to their well-functioning moral compass, they move.*

This is what my friend chose to do. He responded tenderly, mercifully, patiently, lovingly, forgivingly, and kindly. He did this all while facing a great threat to himself and to his family's future. There was no map app with navigation instructions. No one he knew had faced something like this, and nothing about it made sense.

It didn't have to.

His commitment was *to do right.*

Courageous leaders have learned to govern themselves, to manage their emotional reactivity, and to restrain their impulsivity.

There is probably no more spectacular example than Jesus in Gethsemane. [Matthew 26:36-46]

Entering the garden, Jesus is feeling the weight of the immense spiritual battle bearing down upon him. So, he asks his three most dependable, most intimate friends to stand with him in prayer. After a short time he returns to find them asleep. "Couldn't you watch with me one hour?" he asks. "Watch and pray so that you will not fall into temptation. The spirit is willing, but the flesh is weak."

Do you hear him begging them? Expressing bitter disappointment in them? I don't.

I hear him calling them to do what's right in that very intense moment. He also uses their failure as an opportunity to teach them about spiritual warfare. It will serve them later.

Jesus resumes warring in prayer alone. Scripture records that, being in anguish, he prayed more earnestly, and his sweat was like drops of blood falling to the ground. [Luke 22:44] I don't know what all that means *other than* his struggle was intense—more than he'd ever experienced. His request in essence is "Father, is there *any other* way? Ok then, your will be done."

In his humanity, wouldn't Jesus have *wanted* a way out? Wouldn't his impulse be to give in? To give up? To escape the burden crushing his soul?

Jesus, our example of self-leadership, restrains his very human impulse to escape the intensity of this assignment, and subordinates his emotional reactivity to his commitment to his Father that would benefit all humanity. It is important to point out that he didn't achieve this *by his own power* or determination. Coming to the end of himself, Jesus cries out to the Father who sends an angel. The angel appears to him and strengthens him. [Luke 22:43]

Courageous leaders have learned to govern themselves, to manage their emotional reactivity, to restrain their impulsivity.

Like the impulse for revenge, to employ terrorist tactics, or zero-sum strategies. Courageous leaders will resist the ever-present impulse to resist another's resistance.

Think about that for a minute. When you encounter someone else resisting you, what you stand for, care about, or are invested in what do you do? The most natural thing is for you to resist them back. Right?

I assert you do this all the time.

A few years ago, our ministry team was engaged in intense strategic meetings that would determine the direction of our ministry around the globe. We had the benefit of "fresh eyes" as three millennials had recently joined our team. From their perspective, several of the ministry methods that I'd helped to pioneer over more than a decade were grossly outdated, even misguided based on their understanding of scripture. My opportunity, in that moment, was to remind myself that my value and security were safely in the Father's arms. Postured this way, I could remain curious and give careful consideration to their perspectives.

Instead, I childishly interpreted their observations as criticisms of my cherished contributions to our work. My interpretation that these were personal rebukes fueled my angry, impassioned response.

Instead, a self-differentiated leader will surrender herself to integrity. Her integrity. She entrusts herself to God, being obedient as best she can, to what she knows to be right.

A Christian leader cannot afford to be reactive as I was. Nor can he be capricious, impetuous, or mercurial. If he is, those he leads cannot follow. Leaders are only leaders *when* people follow.

It's incumbent upon leaders in the Church to do what we know to be right. Because, when we don't, we compromise ourselves. When you compromise your own integrity, you commit moral suicide.

When you fail to do what you know to be right, you immediately lose esteem for yourself. The antidote to low self-esteem is not the empty pumping up of those who live without integrity. *It is to live a life that you yourself esteem.* A life that you respect. To quote my friend, you do what's right.

One tragedy of Christian leadership in our day is that far too many suffer from this malady. Collapsing on what they know to be right, the erosion of esteem begins its inexorable advance.

Confidence is undermined. One collapse breeds another.

Compromised, the leader looks outside to determine direction. Like the politician taking cues from polling data, she's straining to sense the political winds rather than standing on the moral certitude of doing the right thing.

The question is no longer "what is *right?*" but "what'll *work?*" Adrift of one's ethical moorings, the tragedies mount.

This is what passes for leadership in a culture of cowardice.

What if the Church in our nation determined to do what we know to be right, simply because it *is* right? What if honor and integrity supplanted expediency and political advantage?

How might we then live?

How might our society respond?

FOR PERSONAL REFLECTION:

Reflect on the account of the US Marines landing on Peleliu as depicted in *The Pacific*.

- What about the posture, discipline, and behavior of the officers is most striking to you?
- When you've been "under fire" recently how would you assess the way you carried yourself?
- If you could live that situation over again, what would you do differently?
- Jesus often devoted prolonged periods to prayer in solitude. How well have your prayer habits supported you when "enemy fire" has come against you?
- How well have your prayer habits supported you when those you lead have come under attack?

FOR GROUP DISCUSSION:

- Discuss your organization's willingness for people to "take the first step," particularly when there is danger and the outcome is uncertain?
- Why do you think this is?
- What could be done to adopt an ethos where "going first" is the most likely response to opportunities?
- Discuss why you think Jesus preached as he did in John 6:30-65. What was his purpose?
- When would it make sense for your ministry or organization to communicate a "hard word" like Jesus did here?

PART FOUR

CODA

You were made to lead. To influence. To be a role model for your church, organization, or system. As American culture becomes less tolerant of evangelical Christianity (and *everything* Christian for that matter) it is all the more important that pastors and leaders surrender to the reality that they are made to lead.

That you feel inadequate for such a role is not surprising. *It is exactly how God works with honest women and men.* Throughout scripture, God repeatedly places those he loves in perilous conditions where, apart from God's intervention, they cannot possibly rise to the task. Yet, they do. Trusting God, they leap. When they don't, God works in or through their example to instruct the rest of us.

Doesn't he?

Edwin Friedman provides such a clear picture of effective leadership: self-defined, connected to people, and non-anxious while immersed in the societal disquiet produced by chronic anxiety. Jesus lived this before us. His example is captured in scripture, as is that of dozens of Old and

New Testament leaders. I assert that these women and men were almost as strongly predisposed to cowardice as you and I are.

Yet, they often summoned the courage God had deposited in them, trusted him against the odds, and, according to Romans 11:33-40 they conquered kingdoms, administered justice, gained what was promised, shut the mouths of lions, quenched the fury of flames, and escaped the edge of the sword. Their weakness was turned to strength; they became powerful in battle and routed opposing armies. Women received their dead, raised to life again. Others were tortured, refusing to be released so that they might gain an even better resurrection. Many faced jeers and floggings, chains, and imprisonment. They were put to death by stoning, sawed in two, killed by the sword. They traveled about in sheepskins and goatskins, destitute, persecuted and mistreated, wandering in deserts and mountains, living in caves and in holes in the ground. Of these, the author of Hebrews says: "The world was not worthy."

In our day, *we are the ones who get to live valiantly*, demonstrating what it is to trust God and leap. *We* are the ones who get to live this way—not just on occasion when our carefully scripted plans are upended by the unanticipated. We get to live this way routinely, as a matter of course, because it's the way we've chosen. The God way.

But, I'm a "chicken."

So are you. Our conscious and subconscious minds are continually scanning our surroundings to identify threats *to avoid them*. Trouble is, indulge this too effectively and we're stuck. Rutted. Trapped and, in that frame of living, we don't grow. To *ever* leap in life is to behave counter-intuitively.

Before I knew Jesus, I was a student at Purdue. My buddy Scott Waters and I stood on the edge of a cliff seventy feet above the crystal-clear spring water of France Park's granite quarry. Our girlfriends, Annie and Anne, watched from below. They were far too smart to attempt something so potentially dangerous—and exciting. I remember standing there, the sun's warmth on my shoulders, the breeze moving against my skin, the discomfort of the loose gravel on the tiny stone outcropping pressing into my bottoms of my feet. There I stood, squinting my eyes, trying to focus on the ripples on the lake below.

Would I jump?

I *had to* jump! Scott was ready to jump. Heck, *Scott was always ready to jump!* And, the girls were watching, waiting, staring up into the afternoon sun.

To leap, I would have to suspend everything I'd trained myself to think and feel in the face of a potential hazard like that. But Annie was watching, and Scott was waiting, so I took a deep breath and heaved myself into the air.

Ten years later, I was on my skis in Jackson Hole, staring into the gaping crevasse of terror that is Corbet's Couloir. Shaped like an upside-down funnel, a thin ribbon of snow divides pitiless walls of rock no more than ten feet apart. Oh, and to enter, I'd have to drop, airborne, about fifteen feet from the cornice where I stood. Then I'd have to break my descent and hope to make an immediate jump turn before being plastered on the north rock face. *That's why* Corbet's is known as "America's scariest ski slope."

"Oh, Jesus," I *prayed.*

Quickly, I sized up the situation. I was an expert skier *and* after decades skiing in the Alps, the Rockies, Tetons, Laurentians, Wasatch, and the Green Mountains, I'd never seen *anything* this intimidating. We had three children at home. A fourth was due in September. No way was I going to put my family, myself, and my body at risk for something so meaningless as this! My heart pounding, I dug my poles into the wind-packed overhang of snow, and pushed back from the edge. I finished the week on the more orthodox exhilaration provided by the Hobacks and Rendezvous Bowl.

I'm arguing that leaders leap. Trusting God, we throw our bodies into the spiritual couloirs of ministry and life *for the sake of Jesus' mission: the Father's Kingdom*. It would've been foolish for me to attempt to conquer Corbet's. My body is no longer my own to use impulsively. [1 Corinthians 6:19]. In 2 Corinthians 5:15, Paul writes: "...he died for all, that those who live should no longer live for themselves but for him who died for them and was raised again." Our lives are to be submitted to God's will and ways. This, I assert, will produce a heroic, God-honoring way of life.

Another decade later, we were reeling. The new church Annie and I had poured ourselves into, as you've already read, had broken apart after an affair destroyed the marriages of our two most visible leaders. Sitting in a pastors' conference in Wheatridge, Colorado, I sensed God's direction to leave Indiana, get an M.Div., and to intern at a healthy, established church where we'd relocate. With six kids, a budding business, and decades of committed friendships, it would take a courageous leap to obey God.

Almost immediately I hired a Greek tutor (I'm *awful* with languages), and I started researching suitable seminaries with churches near them. Then we began laying the groundwork for so momentous a move: our family's first. God graced us with connections to faculty members, pastors, advisers, and people willing to open their hearts and lives to us. Inside a year I was at Fuller Theological Seminary and living in Orange County. The kids were situated in two Christian schools, and I'd been generously invited to join the staff of the Newport Vineyard.

A few months after our arrival the perilousness of the faith leap we'd undertaken began to reveal itself. All of us struggled with culture shock. We had moved from the simplicity and stability of a small, conservative city in Indiana to the affluence, decadence, and deeply embedded self-indulgence of life in Southern California. The business I'd built in Indiana collapsed within a year of our move providing unanticipated financial pressures. Our marriage wobbled as I withdrew into school, ministry, and trying to rescue the business, leaving Annie alone to deal with her loss of place. Add to that the emerging disturbance of our newly-minted adolescents exploring the largely parentless world of their exciting new friends. What followed were school suspensions, explorations with sex, alcohol, and drugs, late nigh phone calls from the police, court dates, and jail time.

These difficulties eventually drove me to Jesus, into therapy, coaching, and intensive work on my character. The result is a journey that placed *A Failure of Nerve* in my hands exactly when I needed it.

Whatever setbacks you've encountered were not intended to harm your fruitfulness in Christ. God's intent through them is to *make a Christian out of you!* As with me. I was following Jesus but not living like him—at least not nearly enough to be self-defined and non-anxious when disquiet was ever-present.

I remember being terrified. Very late one night in 1978, my friend Hal West was visiting me in Boston. We were waiting in the dirty, urine-soaked, graffiti-stained South Station subway stop for our train. Three or four dangerous-looking thugs were eyeing us. When we were finally alone on the platform, they approached menacingly. We were in danger.

Moving toward us, they began to mock threateningly. I don't remember who said it first, but both Hal and I began to exclaim: "the blood of Jesus, the blood of Jesus, the *blood* of Jesus!" At first, it was a whispered prayer, spoken under our breaths. But, continuing, we spoke more loudly and urgently *at our attackers.*

Hal and I'd had some experience with "spiritual warfare," including praying for the liberation of people oppressed by spiritual forces. We'd seen the potency of reminding principalities and powers that while on our own, *we* were easy prey. But we stood in the name of Jesus because of the sacrifice he made on our behalf. At that moment, we stepped toward our adversaries (I actually don't know why) and proclaimed that we were protected by Jesus' blood. After a few steps, our attackers stopped advancing. One shouted, "Hey man, they're saying 'the blood of Jesus!'" Frightened, *they* ran off.

Back then, I'd not discovered the principles offered in this book. What I did know is that the only way to stay non-anxious is to hide myself in Christ. God *is* our ever-present help in the midst of trouble. [Psalm 46:1]

In 2014 I was involved in a horrible auto accident. A motorcyclist died and through what was later revealed to be an intentional manipulation of our justice system, I was charged with manslaughter. Then I was sued for $50,000,000. The weight of the grief, coupled with the impending bankruptcy was immense. Then, while biking in Chicago, I was struck by a bus, breaking two ribs and my clavicle. At the same time, one of my sons was losing a decade-long battle with heroin addiction. He was "gone" on what turned out to be a three-week bender we didn't know he'd survive.

In the blackness of that season, God held our heads above water. Hiding myself in him and forcing myself to lock my gaze on Jesus' loving, forgiving, confident face, *I did* employ the principles I learned from Edwin Friedman. All through that harrowing time, I continued to coach and equip pastors across the country to lead themselves and their congregations well. They say my example illustrated the principles that have guided our work.

THESE PRINCIPLES IN PRACTICE

My perch as a leadership coach has provided an excellent vantage point to watch pastors in action. I see them employ the postures and practices offered in this book while leading their congregations in real-time. Let's look at the nine principles with real-life examples that I hope will encourage you.

1. Courageous Leadership is not about Skill, Technique, or Knowledge. It is, most of all, about the Presence of the Leader as he or she Moves through Life

While pastoring an independent evangelical church in a small Oregon town, Sean Flannery began to relate to me that he was sensing God drawing him toward the beauty and transcendence he'd begun to experience in a sacramental context. Over the next months and years, Sean followed as Jesus led him through the Anglican ordination process. As his congregation moved toward becoming an Anglican parish hundreds of conversations were required. Why this change? Why now? What does it mean? What about how we've always done things?

As they approached these crucial conversations, they took a posture of *invitation.* The invitation to dance. Sean and Melody learned that leadership requires that we "dance our people across the dance floor." We don't stand on the far side and demand that they join us. (This insight came from Happy Leman, a mentor, and Pastor of the Vineyard Church of Central Illinois). There was no insistence that the congregation follow them on their episcopal journey. They were not asking permission of their members. God had indicated where Melody and Sean were to lead, and they were moving in obedience. Confident in who they were in Christ, they gave dozens of invitations and watched how people responded.

The changes have been monumental and challenge the way every member relates to God, engages in worship, practices their faith, and understands their place in the Body of Christ. All this while church polity, finances, governance, and ministry structures have been transformed. Through the journey, Sean and Melody stayed close to Jesus *and* close to their people. My observation is that Sean's authentic pursuit of Jesus, clear self-definition amid that quest, and anxiety-quelling presence enabled his members to make the transition. And they were able to do so without infighting that could have led to a catastrophic church split.

For its entire history, the ministry team on which I serve has successfully partnered with mid-level denominational execs. who became champions of our process in their ministry sphere. When the "Great Recession" struck in 2007 it rendered that winning strategy obsolete in sudden, painful, and dramatic fashion. With stunning clarity and peace that can only come from his intimate association with Jesus, David Zimmerman led the team to examine our entire ministry. In particular, we reviewed our service delivery system to determine what was and was no longer working.

He *knew* there was a way for our ministry to strengthen pastors and churches faithfully, but none of us had any idea what that could be.

For the next four years, David calmly led as we prayerfully reinvented first "the why" and then "the how" of our ministry. If he was caught up in our organizational anxiety, it was not apparent. What did show was his deep connection to us, our cause, and the God he believed was leading us even when we couldn't see where that was. His presence mollified our disquiet, even when *I* became fearful and angry.

With the help of consultants, we undertook a StratOp process in late 2012. The following year was devoted to developing new training resources, conceiving and writing a radical, fresh business plan, and innovating our new way forward. David participated flexibly and devotedly throughout the process, encouraging us and engaging our participation along the path. We piloted our new approach at his church in Atlanta.

The pilot was a fairly abysmal failure. Calmly, he led us to debrief the pilot experience which provided the fuel to make steady improvements over the next year. By 2015, the ministry had the first of what has now been several consecutive years of unprecedented fruitfulness, ministry growth, and effectiveness. It wasn't David's skill, technique, or knowledge that was so helpful to our navigating the unknown. It was his God-trusting presence with and among us.

2. Take Full Responsibility for your own Emotional Being and Destiny

When I began coaching Kristy Turner, she was pastoring a fairly conventional Vineyard church in an affluent Florida community. The church was stable, free of turmoil, financially solid. She acknowledged a growing dissatisfaction with teaching Christianity to mature Christians, putting on weekend events, and continually comforting her people. As we explored this dissonance over several months, a burden for an economically-challenged community a few miles away became clear. So, she began to lead a team from her church to minister to residents of an apartment complex there that God seemed to direct them toward. The response was heartening. People became open to the Gospel and received Kristy and her team with sincerity and trust. At the same time, influential members of her church began to oppose the ministry "over there."

As she sought the Lord, she sensed God's leading to relocate the church where the new converts could be enfolded, cared for, and discipled. Once a location was identified, and most of the financing was secured her influential antagonists became more strident. Their giving dried up. Several left the church taking many with them. Through this difficult time, Kristy continued to draw close to the Lord, experiencing God's sustenance and strength as she did. She determined not to retaliate when people assailed her leadership, character, and vision.

Kristy chose not to make the struggle about her rivals, but to interpret it as a normal, though non-ideal, response to unwanted change. Ultimately, the impact on giving was too great for the church to survive. As she made the courageous decision to close the church, she and her team continued to serve the unchurched and sought opportunities to minister in her giftings. I admire the way Kristy exemplified what it means to take full responsibility before God for her own being and destiny, particularly in the midst of backlash.

Michael White, when I met him, had recently been called to pastor a mid-sized Baptist church in a California mountain town. He may have described both the congregation and community as "sleepy" upon his arrival. What was delightful was the church's love for Jesus and one another. What was disturbing was the immense inward focus of the church's programming, ethos, and culture. Like many good churches in America, they were great at, and greatly satisfied with, caring for themselves. Michael, though, had other ideas. His vision was for this church to effectively and consistently serve the non-Christians in the community. As they served, the church would become an essential part of the community's relational and practical infrastructure.

He began communicating this vision in every context he could think of: pulpit, with community leaders, elders' meetings, and lay leader gatherings. *As is always the case*, this was met with both enthusiasm and derision from key influencers inside. Working with the most amenable, Michael made steady progress seeding the conversations his members were having all the time. But, when the most influential and enduring elder—who was the new pastor's greatest advocate—suddenly died, the congregation entered a prolonged season of deep mourning. As it did, it turned inward with unbridled determination.

Michael went out into the community and began to establish friendships with community leaders and people who frequented local stores, shops, restaurants, and bars, community organizations, and non-profits. Taking full responsibility for his own emotional being and destiny, he chose to overlook, as much as possible, the acrimony of members determined to sustain the congregation's inward focus. Collaborating with those who shared his passion to minister outside, a key staff member and lay leadership team took the church through the Missional Pathway. It was a nearly year-long process to discover God's unique missional purpose for individuals and the congregation as a whole. Soon, a team was ministering at a local public school, supporting faculty, staff, and students.

The new endeavor enlivened the congregation who were proud that their church was helping improve the lives of those outside. Soon they became known for the good that was being accomplished for the sake of the school family. Michael, following a life-long passion, began to volunteer with the High School baseball program. Players and coaches met Jesus, and the affirmations from the community greeted Michael and his people all over town.

Throughout the transition, Michael was assisted by the deep-rooted conviction that *God* wanted him to foster meaningful bonds with people far from Jesus, but close to him. And, by investing his time, attention, and energy almost exclusively in those who wanted to see the church impact the community, he benefited from the camaraderie of impassioned, like-minded believers. He avoided the malady so common to other pastors of having their ambition and momentum sapped by the faithless whining of faint-hearted church members.

3. Promote Healthy Differentiation within the Church or System you Lead

My friend Sam serves as an intentional interim pastor in a large Presbyterian denomination. Our coaching relationship has spanned stints at churches in Georgia, New Jersey, and Florida. From Sam I learned that interims are ideal openings to promote healthy differentiation in the churches he serves. In fact, he might say it is the *most important* task of an interim.

In Sam's denomination, there is often a period approaching two years between lead pastors. Some of this is search process time, but most of it is a time for what Sam calls "intentional differentiation training." He uses this time to advance the Christian maturity of Session members, lay leaders, and the search committee—pointing them to Jesus and scripture in the midst of sometimes severe uncertainty and distress. In the interim ambiguity, differentiation training has at least two key impacts:

Sometimes, members employ blame and scapegoating to make sense of the former pastor's departure. So, Sam works to provide perspective, promote forgiveness, and to cultivate personal responsibility for each person's contribution to recent church conflicts or disappointments. He walks with community members so they can better recognize how they may have played a part in the pastor's exodus and impacted the ways they've been in relationship with one another.

Congregations and leaders often feel paralyzed—helpless to move forward courageously or live mission faithfully unless and until the new pastor arrives. This state leads to anxious searches for magic bullet pastors and congregational expectations that no human can meet. Differentiation helps members recognize the calling, gifts, and power of God resident in and at work through them long after the former pastor departed, and before their next pastor arrives. A differentiated congregation is better equipped to create a healthy partnership with its next pastor rather than an anxious undifferentiated codependency!

Sam is quietly confident that God is sovereignly at work in the call process. He also recognizes that the congregation is privileged to walk forward until that choice is revealed. These may be the two most influential aspects of his role. In the waiting, he works to reinterpret the churches' history through the lens of a loving, attentive God working for their good [Romans 8:28] no matter how events appear to be at the time.

Because of the accumulated experience he has with many churches, he carries a confidence that God will provide at just the right moment. Before that happens, the congregation's job is to prepare: to become as non-anxious and self-differentiated as possible before the new leader arrives.

It's been a joy to coach the planters of an independent church to serve urban Las Vegas' working poor. Modeled after the sending church in another state, they did tremendous work bringing people to Christ. They help folks grow in the rudiments of the faith and establish and support ministry leaders while they remain focused on community engagement through partnership with the City by serving the homeless.

After a few years, they caught the attention of a trendy, vibrant church movement looking to expand into their city. Carefully Julian and Demi (not their real names) evaluated the culture, ministry philosophy, vision, and strategy of the adopting movement, then prayerfully considered the opportunity to shift from independence to become a local expression of this international collection of churches.

Along the way, they challenged their leaders to seek the Lord's direction for them individually and corporately. Once the decision was made to accept the offer, *everyone's* role had to change. The responsibilities, reporting relationships, duties, and routines that had become comfortably familiar to their team became ambiguous overnight.

Sunday services were suspended to make room for each person to activate their "Christ-centric muscles." They did this by individually pursuing Jesus and by forming meaningful relationships with the unchurched in their spheres of influence. Julian understood that if they swiftly rushed into weekend services—which is the expectation of most churchgoers today—it would only serve to fortify the greater culture's pervasive consumer mentality.

Julian used the respite from putting on the public services to provide comprehensive leadership equipping.

For some, anxiety dominated. Others found the uncertainty exciting. A few influential leaders were overwhelmed by the challenge of change and exited the adventure. Demi and Julian kept pointing people to Jesus, their Rock in the midst of uncertainty. Rather than identifying with the weekend event, people were encouraged to drive their roots deep in Christ, growing in personal prayer and scripture study. In this way, the DNA of the new enterprise was "set" in people's personal pursuit of Jesus and their neighbors.

4. Stand, as an Exemplar, in the Sabotage and Backlash that Must Come

I've found Diego (not his real name) to be one of the most coachable pastors I've had the privilege to work with. When we met, his brief tenure at a traditional, old-line church just South of Los Angeles was difficult. He desired to lead a congregation that was bringing people to faith and actively ministering to those in need in the neighborhoods nearby. Early on, his sharing about these passions received quiet acquiescence from the greying congregation. But, as soon as he attempted to lead them to take action, hostility emerged. When the elders requested that Diego resign, he didn't. So, *they* quit. His entire board eventually left the church, prompting others to exit, resulting in a swirl of blame and confusion.

In dozens of difficult conversations, Diego invited his people to put their trust in Jesus. He encouraged them with the promises of God and pointed them to God's design that the Church be salt and light in the community. [Matthew 5:13-16] When a season of unremitting criticism directed at his leadership and character caused his confidence to shudder, Diego grounded himself in God's faithfulness to him *and to them.* He reminded himself that, while he may have had a contribution to whatever troubled his critics, he was neither their cause nor responsible for their solution. He became adept at directing people to the Lord Jesus. And, he took his own advice!

All this time Diego continued to lead. He assembled a team that went off campus to serve residents and staff at a senior living facility. Whenever he could, Diego took members to minister with him. Initially, though, he frequently went alone, or with his wife Ana (not her real name) and their children. Before long at the Care Center, pervading joy replaced dreariness as residents enjoyed stimulating conversation, found meaningful connection, and the staff received encouraging assistance. The administration began to have hope once again. When I visited, people lit up as Diego and Ana entered each room, where they were greeted with hugs and smiles. As residents, family members, and employees gave their lives to Jesus, members of the church were reenergized, their faith refreshed for the first time in decades.

After a few years, the church had multiplied their ministries to those outside. Many young couples found their way into the church, and a solid and supportive leadership infrastructure shouldered the load with a grateful pastor. Diego has faced many more challenges than I've described. Diego stood as an example to his people—even his decriers. Being settled on the unwavering faithfulness of God served Diego throughout the nine years we've walked together. As he's grown in Christlikeness, he's provoked maturity in those around him.

When we began coaching together, Andy was pastoring the English-speaking congregation within a large Mandarin church in a suburban California community. Leadership on the Chinese side was initially supportive of his efforts to equip and lead his people to minister in the community. Over time, Andy's team began to focus their ministry efforts at a community center that served Chinese immigrants nearby, until pushback from church leadership undermined those efforts. Undaunted, Andy built a solid and ardent cadre of ministry leaders to pioneer relationships with the unchurched with whom they shared a common culture. Momentum was increasing as their congregation grew healthier, deeply connected, and influential outside.

Then, church elders adopted a ministry philosophy that could not have been further from Andy's. The message was communicated with unmistakable clarity: "Ministry and ministry activity is to be concentrated here at the church. You are not to leave the campus during your work week." After repeated attempts to negotiate an amenable middle ground, Andy reluctantly submitted his resignation.

Over a tumultuous period of weeks, a team organically formed around him. They met to dream about what God had begun in them and how it might play out. Andy stood. Without a church, position, or salary, he stood. Somehow, support came both practically and financially. After a period of "wilderness wandering" Andy and his team merged with a church that shared their vision and values. All this time, he devoted himself to prayer and the ongoing formation of his people as disciples of Jesus and ministers of the Gospel.

The team drew strength from Andy's example of calm reliance on God in the midst of encircling uncertainty. As I write this, they're multiplying missional communities that are united in growth, outwardly-focused ministry, and fellowship.

5. Don't "Push on the Rope:" the Unmotivated are Invulnerable to Insight

Like most pastors, Kevin Walkowiak is a kindhearted man. We met at a pastors' conference outside Houston when he was in his late thirties. What distinguished Kevin to me was his desire to lead a church that *made a difference.* He'd grown tired of purveying religious education and entertainment to deeply committed Christian people. "What about impacting our *city?*", he asked. Learning about the Missional Pathway, Kevin seemed intrigued. Here was a process designed to walk his churches through the steps to redemptive community impact.

Kevin shared his desire to engage the Pathway with both elder boards, but the response was mixed. Several had little interest in "that missional business" holding to the traditional priority that a pastors' focus is to be on the care, comfort, and education of church members. Others, however, were thrilled. While no one knew *how* the process would go, these were willing to leap together, trusting God. Many of this second group were not part of either congregation's established leaders. Kevin determined to center his time, energy, and attention on these, and while he loved and cared for the rest, moved out into mission without them.

Whether he knew it or not, in one decisive move, he prevented much heartache (both for himself and others), hours of meaningless cajoling and arm-twisting, and the achingly slow forward progress that characterized most every innovation he'd attempted to that point.

As Kevin and his "pioneers" proceeded together, God directed them to a city official who facilitated a connection to "the 805," a previously overlooked neighborhood where his members now care for, encourage, connect, and provide practical service to grateful residents each week, year-round. As word of their groundbreaking ministry spread, local firefighters joined Kevin's team. Officials in other parts of the metro area are pondering ways to replicate what Kevin's team has accomplished.

Doug (not his real name), as Associate Pastor of a large suburban church, has been tasked with leading a number of systemic change initiatives that affect virtually every aspect of the Presbyterian Church he serves. While working to rally support from decision-makers, enroll and equip leaders to share the stewardship, and identify and train volunteers, he's realized that there is a "church within the church."

Much of the congregation is delighted to participate in church life as they have for their lifetimes. Rather than agonizing over ways to move the unmovable, Doug has chosen to share the pastoral team's vision and listen for those who both want the same things *and* are willing to help it happen. Recognizing that *people always self-select*, he's found those who are passionate for the endeavors he cares most about and works with them. In the process, they enjoy camaraderie and fruitfulness while minimizing the energy-sapping conversations about why this or that won't work, shouldn't be attempted, or hasn't been done here before.

Doug cares greatly about discipleship: believers maturing in Christ-like character regardless of their starting point. Since he's convinced that he can't "push on a rope," he focuses his energy on those most open to his influence. As a result, he and they experience progress more quickly than if he were cheerleading people who don't share Doug's hunger to grow.

Employing this principle, he has mobilized a robust lay ministry team that is presencing the Gospel among staff, residents, and family members at a residential facility for seniors near his church. Several times each week, church members are over at the senior center caring for, encouraging, listening to, and befriending the elderly residents. As they do, they bring Jesus with them.

6. Undermine the 80/20 Rule

Leading a city-wide ministry coordinating the efforts of dozens of short-term teams for the Southern Baptists provided Jay Schroder abundant opportunities to over-function *or* to champion others to shoulder the burden of leadership with him. In my view, Jay succeeded spectacularly. First, he assembled a team of summer interns through whom he coordinated the projects of more than a thousand volunteers who descended on Northern Ohio each summer. Then he intentionally built his interns as leaders, investing months in their development well before the arrival of the teams.

Rather than simply cataloging and evaluating work projects proposed by local pastors and church planters, Jay sowed into their development as well. The pastors and planters were diverse: white, black, Hispanic, and Asian. They spoke English, Spanish, Chinese, Arabic, and even sign language, and they came from suburban, urban, downtown, up-and-coming, and some of the worst neighborhoods in Greater Cleveland. Intentionally undermining the 80/20 Rule, Jay worked to grow them as leaders.

Helping them identify God's handprints on their desires and gifts, Jay greatly expanded their investment in and commitment to crucial relational opportunities that the work projects would strengthen—not define. Thinking well beyond 80/20, Jay sought to change the way the pastors and planters ministered in their neighborhoods all year long.

Typically, summer mission teams prefer to visit a new city each year, to provide a vacation-like experience for their volunteers. Jay persuaded several teams to make long-term commitments to Cleveland, deepening their own development and the Kingdom-advancing impact their repeated presence could have.

When the teams came into town, Jay and his assistants made sure they weren't focused on pounding nails, finishing concrete, and applying paint. Experiences, exercises, debrief discussions, and practices were built into the volunteers' schedule to weld their service to Kingdom ministry and to their advancement as apprentices of Jesus. Jay evaluated each person as a potential leader, often thrusting them into responsibilities earlier than their own church may have suggested. With support, encouragement, and intentional development, leadership gaffes were rare, and when they happened were powerful learning experiences for the summer volunteers.

Feedback from the volunteers, pastors and church planters with whom the teams partnered, and Jay's leadership team confirmed the deep transformational impact of their time together, whether it spanned days, months, or years.

Kit Rae is the only example in this section of the book that I've not yet had the privilege to coach. And, his is my favorite example of undermining our propensity in church life to promote "80/20" by intention or accident. As campus pastor for rockharbor Costa Mesa, where Annie and I attended for many wonderful years, his bold innovation and leadership have impacted eternity for thousands. Here's what I mean.

Our church had a big and successful VBS that always had a cool theme, amazing visuals, loads of energy, and was lots and lots of fun. And, the kids—almost all of whom were from churched families—grew in their understanding of Jesus and the Bible. In one bold, risky, and unpopular stroke, Kit changed all that.

Rather than locating VBS as we always had, in our more than ample church facilities, Kit proposed that we move it off-campus. This year, we'd take VBS to where the kids of Orange County are: to *their* neighborhoods, back yards, garages, parks, club houses, and community centers. Kit's appeal: if you can host a birthday party for your own kids, you can host a VBS! We offered VBS at thirty sites.

To succeed, Kit's staff team had to undergo a fundamental shift in their responsibilities. Instead of doing the ministry themselves, the staff coached and supported hundreds of nervous and excited lay ministers. To pull off something this big, they had to recruit and equip several times the number of adult and teen volunteers as in previous years. And, by design, church staff did not host, run, or work any of the sites. It was 100% lay ministry.

Kit knew that when Christians commit to minister for the benefit of others, *they would be changed by God.* What I'm not sure he knew was that a thousand kids would participate in VBS that year and that 90% would come from unchurched families. Up to that point, just like at your church, our Vacation Bible School attracted 80% church kids. Every year since, under Kit's leadership, this essential ministry has been offered *out there*: where the kids who need Jesus most are. As it has, Ephesians 4:11-13 has been lived out: hundreds of Christians have been flung into a powerful, risky, life-on-life ministry that's changed their relationship with Jesus and their neighborhoods forever. He reports that the experience grew the people, stretched their faith, increased their dependence on Jesus, and allowed them to see God move in real and tangible ways. Kit knew that unlike conventional VBS when this week was over, the ministry in the neighborhoods would continue... and it has to this day!

7. Disengage from an Unreasonable Faith in Reasonableness

When I met Mike Wilson, he was pastoring a Wesleyan church in an urban setting in the Midwest. There, he initiated several exciting ministries for and among those in the city. It was thrilling to hear about people giving their lives to Jesus and growing in their newfound faith. At the same time, structural changes and financial pressures in his denominational hierarchy necessitated that his church be closed.

Mike took a call to an independent, rural Bible church that had been rocked by a series of pastoral scandals. Despite the severity of the struggles, most in the church maintained a deep allegiance to the previous pastor and were openly hostile toward Mike. Mike set out to meet with as many of his decriers as he could, hear their views and, as best he could, respond to their growing list of objections to his leadership style, preaching, ministry priorities, and personality. As we discussed these many painful encounters, it became clear that—as is so often the case—the criticisms were neither reasonable nor rational. This vocal majority was relentlessly, emotionally committed to having "their church" and "their pastor" back. There was no reasoning with those who were determined to overlook the very disturbing failings of the founding pastor while only finding fault with Pastor Mike and his wife.

Interrupting his preference to labor to find common ground with his detractors, Mike turned his attention to those willing to follow his lead. Taking a page from the playbook at his former church, he built relationships with many community leaders, volunteered on committees, and labored alongside those who cared for those in need in the county. Eventually, others from the church joined him. As Mike continued to preach the scriptures clearly and unapologetically, guests began to visit. In time, many came to faith in Christ and were baptized. A fresh wind of God's Spirit had begun to blow. Many were blessed. Others, including *all* those who were devoted to the previous pastor, raised a ruckus, stopped giving, sent emails to the members threatening to leave if Mike wasn't replaced. Eventually, they found their way to other churches. All of them.

In his mid-thirties, Dan is a Free Methodist pastor in a major metropolitan area. Apostolic by gifting, he is always starting exciting new works, connecting with civic leaders, dreaming up innovative ways to engage the lost, and pushing just about every envelope in sight. The executive team at his district office has noticed Dan's work and been more than a little enthusiastic about the ministry innovation. With their approval, Dan's church leased space and opened a social enterprise cafe as a gathering place for area residents. In cooperation with local non-profits, disadvantaged young adults receive life-transforming mentoring, job training, and employment at the shop. Meaningful community events are held every month, ministry takes place there every day, and the local neighbors love it! After a year, it's been a tremendous success by every measure but one.

Finances have always been a struggle. When the district decided not to assist further with any of their ample finances, Dan found a business tenant with complimentary operating hours to sublet the space. When that arrangement was suddenly terminated, Dan was back at the district office asking for help.

Ever positive and encouraging, they asked for a detailed business plan. Dan and his team complied, after which months of back-and-forth conversations took place. Addressing each objection, answering loads of questions, Dan continued to reason with the decision-makers who had the resources and autonomy to invest deeply in this missional ministry endeavor. As before, they decided to watch and wait, while Dan and his intrepid venture continues to rely on financial support from his church.

Finally determined to stop reasoning with what I, as Dan's coach, consider the "systemic cowardice" of denominational administrators, he's creating associations and raising investment from civic and business organizations who, like Dan, are taking risks to improve and develop their beleaguered neighborhoods. It is working! Though the pressures are enormous, Dan is no longer placing "an unreasonable faith in reasonableness" but he is joining visionaries like himself who are bettering lives while making Jesus' presence unavoidable in East Pasadena.

8. Reintroduce Yourself to the Adventurous Life

Tim Eaton's entire tenure at Edgewater Lutheran Church has been an adventure. Leaving a staff position at a well-established church, Tim planted the LCMS church in a recently incorporated section of Southern California's sprawling Inland Empire. The founders of the church envisioned traditional Sunday services and congregational gatherings for the faithful who'd relocated for the new and affordable housing. Tim had been faithfully providing what I refer to as "religious education and entertainment" for church members. When we met at a coffee shop in 2012 he was unnerved by the question: "If Edgewater were to suddenly close, would anybody outside the congregation notice? Would *those outside* experience loss?"

Tim admitted that the church had no consistent presence in the community. They'd handed out water bottles a few times, yet there was no evidence they'd made any impact. His passion was to ensure that Edgewater was *effective* ministering in and to the community around them. He said: "I don't just want to do Sunday mornings. I want to affect lives." With this, another adventure began.

First, he labored to find and articulate a vision worth giving his life for. It became clear that his heart is to see families transformed, so they walk with confidence and love each other in powerfully positive community. He longed to see "transformed families transforming other families."

Almost immediately, Tim's wife leaped into the adventure by launching a daycare in their home to forge growing relationships with local families. Then Tim led the congregation in a year-long process to discover and clarify God's unique calling to each member—and the congregation as a whole—to live as missionaries locally. Sensing God's direction, they began to invest regularly and personally in the lives of the faculty, administration, and staff at the elementary school where the church met for worship.

They experimented with faculty appreciation lunches, helping teachers set up their classrooms at the start of each semester, providing childcare for date nights for students' parents, hosting movie nights, tutoring students, and making facilities improvements. In every case, the intention is to initiate and strengthen authentic relationship with the school community, showing the goodness of Jesus' Good News, and earning the right to share the Gospel when invited. In a few short years, God has welded an inseparable bond between church and school impacting faculty members and student families.

Jim Duran's entire Christian life has been punctuated by surprising interventions, miraculous provision, and the extension of God's reign among the most vulnerable in Ventura County. Jim was a Foursquare pastor when we began our coaching relationship a few years ago. He'd grown up in the area, had been rescued from addiction in his forties, and witnessed his son's supernatural resuscitation from drowning after underwater for twenty minutes.

Early in his career, Jim worked for a moving company after selling his house cleaning business. During this time, he experimented leading Bible studies. God blessed it as many people came to a first-time faith in Jesus.

Jim became a licensed pastor, and in 2005 the Bible study grew to become The River Community Church.

After eight years in rented spaces, an opportunity came to relocate to the facilities of a declining church. God unexpectedly provided a multi-million-dollar property for The River to call home.

While Lead Pastor of the River, Jim also served on the board of City Center—a struggling transitional living facility. Within two years, the entire Center was filled to capacity as Jim and the River staff provided the leadership, training, manpower, and care that the City Center needed to serve people transitioning out of prison, working toward sobriety, and stabilizing their single-parent families. Then after managing Tender Life Maternity Home for two years, it was sold to the River. Now Jim and the church minister to homeless pregnant mothers. After a child is born, single parents receive up to a year of housing, mentoring, life skills, Christian discipleship, aid navigating a labyrinth of government systems, job placement, and lots of personal care.

Being ushered into leadership of the River, of City Center, and of Tender Life are emblematic of the adventurous life Jim and Pam are living as they simply seek to love and serve the broken and marginalized the way Jesus would. At the time I'm writing this, they've assembled a robust team from the River who have adopted the downtown business association demonstrating the goodness of God to merchants, guests, and visitors to Ventura.

9. Go First!

Wayne is one of my favorite people alive. He loves to say: "Isn't it funny that when we sit down and read our Bibles we don't read about people sitting down and reading their Bibles?" We read about people doing exploits for God! Wayne understands that leaders go. Leaders do.

Leaders act. And leaders take action precisely so that others can observe, be informed, encouraged, and get into action with them. It isn't narcissism to be an intentional role model. It is smart. Strategic. Necessary. Biblical. [1 Corinthians 11:1]

Why did Jesus have the three, the twelve, and the seventy-two? To each, he granted greater access to himself, didn't he? The twelve had more consistent access to and relationship with Jesus than the seventy-two. And the three had an intimacy with Christ that nobody else enjoyed. And, of the three, John experienced a holy closeness unrivaled by any other human.

Leaders go. And they go *before* anybody else. Wayne dreamed of leading a community of people that were so lovingly wed to Jesus and each other, and so committed to growing to maturity that ethnic differences would be irrelevant. So, in 2012 Wayne and Tonja went first. They founded Renewal with a multi-ethnic team from a previous church and merged with an existing church badly needing revitalization. From the outset, the focus has been to grow followers of Jesus Christ who experience healing, equipping, and empowering for service.

Wayne went first, developing and articulating Renewal's mission, vision, values and discipleship strategy, recruiting and leading the ministry leadership team. He designed and implemented a discipleship assessment that helps attendees take the next step in their faith. And he designed a matrix of activities his members can take to grow spiritually.

Sensing an urgency to get the church off its campus to minister to those outside the Faith, Wayne led the implementation of Novo reFocusing's Missional Pathway process, helping each member discover how God prepared them for mission, and coached them as they leaped into ministry as local missionaries. He guided the church as it adopted a public high school where the congregation serves faculty, staff, and students.

As Renewal's principal role model, Wayne goes first. He was part of the first crew of Renewal members who provide snacks and office supplies every Friday morning, to bless teachers and minister to their needs. He's at the high school every Wednesday, developing vital relationships with the principal and assistant principals, engaging students and staff, and discussing the strategic partnership they're building together.

Serving on the staff of an independent evangelical church in Montana, David Halliburton became a coaching client when he accepted the challenge to lead multi-generational family ministries and community ministry in 2010. He was well prepared for this role after serving as Children's Pastor at a large church in California followed by years with YWAM in Thailand, the Philippines, Hawaii, and Montana. He made great progress forging new initiatives in both ministry areas assigned to him.

Then in 2012, David's world collapsed. No one knew that he struggled with an online addiction and had been the victim of sexual abuse when he was young. The former was uncovered when a confidential accountability agreement was betrayed. Staff and elders panicked, and David was fired.

Situations like this happen all across the Church. In virtually every case the dismissed clergyperson moves to a new city, keeps the struggle hidden, and finds another position with a new, unsuspecting church. No one gets healed, nobody gets better, and the devastation grows in the darkness of secrecy.

Going first, David and Elizabeth chose to stay at the church. Before the exposure of David's addiction, they'd lived in secrecy about their struggle. The invitation to seek healing with the loving support of their home church was a powerful and transforming agent. Experiencing grace first hand, they began to model for others that pain is best dealt with in honest vulnerability. They remained in a relationship with the leaders and congregation and pursued extensive counseling, healing, and rehabilitation. Elizabeth returned to the workforce and David held several part-time jobs while they both got as much counseling as they could. While on the path of healing from sexual brokenness, they learned that sex abuse and the secrecy and shame associated with it are pandemic in the U.S.

As David grew in wholeness and health, he served the same church as a layperson, then lay leader. In March 2014, he was invited to rejoin the pastoral staff part-time. As their understanding of recovery ministry had grown David and Elizabeth became clear that God wanted them to minister specifically to the sexually broken, beginning with their home church. Going first, they raised funds and pursued ministry and leadership training with several world-leading ministries specializing in intensive recovery ministry. For the next three years, they traveled to receive thorough training.

By late 2016 they had a clear strategy for "True North 406" the non-profit they would create to provide healing, and leadership training so dozens could join them in caring for the broken hiding in plain sight in churches across the US.

During this time, David led the church through a process to adopt a middle school in an underserved area of their city. David went first, initiating a dynamic partnership between his church and school administrators, enrolling, training, and mobilizing a large team of volunteers who'd come to serve students and faculty every day of the school year.

Today, according to the Principal, David's church has "transformed every aspect of life" at the school, from teacher morale and students' grades to disciplinary problems. True North 406 is conducting twenty-week recovery processes at several churches and is equipping leaders to launch the same process at a half-dozen other churches in the Pacific Northwest.

David and Elizabeth's willingness to "go first," to step into the unknown following Jesus as best they can, has produced the clarity that now punctuates every aspect of their lives both in and outside the vital ministries they lead. In this way they model for hundreds of others what it looks like to step out of the shadows of secrecy and shame into a place of confidence, wellness, and hope.

In Conclusion

So, pastor, what disquiet are you facing?

What "barbarians at the gate" threaten to steal your confidence in Christ?

Could it be that God is at work both to will and to accomplish his good pleasure in you—precisely while you encounter whatever it is you're up against? [Philippians 2:13]

Had the saints we read about in Hebrews 11—based on their present difficulties—decided that God was no longer reliable *I am certain* they'd not have lived so virtuously that, thousands of years later, millions of people would regularly be reminded that "the world was not worthy" of them.

My invitation is simple: ***Join them!***

Leadership Courage Bibliography

Mark Twain: *"Most men die at 27, we just wait to bury them at 72".*

Lewis, CS: The Four Loves

Friedman, Edwin: A Failure of Nerve

St. Irenaeus of Lyons: Against Heresies

Frangipane, Francis: The Three Battlegrounds

Rudy: *"Chasing a stupid dream causes you and everyone around you nothing but heartache..."*

Lewis, CS: The Problem of Pain

Stanley, Andy: The Next Generation Leader

Peterson, Eugene: The Message

Barna, George: Revolution

Friedman, Edwin: Generation to Generation

Novo Mission's reFocusing Team: The Awaken Workshop

Bob Carter: *"Poor planning on your part does not constitute a crisis on my part".*

Goodwin, Bennie: The Effective Leader

Clinton, Dr. J. Robert and Dr. Richard W.: 1991 The Mentor Handbook—Detailed Guidelines and Helps for Christian Mentors and Mentorees. (for Goodwin's Expectation Principle)

Clinton, Dr. J. Robert: Leadership Emergence Theory Manual, Chapter 6, p 208, 209

Flo-TV ad: *"His girlfriend has removed his spine."*

Churchill, Winston, Harrell School, October 1941.

Murrow, David: Why Men Hate Going to Church

Gray, John: Men are from Mars, Women are from Venus

Frederick, Dave: Leaders Book Summaries

New Living Translation

New International Version

The Pacific, HBO miniseries

Gladiator movie

Welch, Jack: *Find out how they keep score… and then score.*

Wimber, John: Signs & Wonders and Church Growth video series

Salucci, Ennio: Reality for a Change

CPSIA information can be obtained
at www.ICGtesting.com
Printed in the USA
LVHW022258020221
678132LV00003B/144